Are You Relevant?

First published by
Thomson-Shore
7300 West Joy Road
Dexter, Michigan 48130

Contact Ross Shafer:
www.RossShafer.com

ISBN: 978-0-615-26523-0

Cover and text design by theBookDesigners

Printed in the United States of America

Are You Relevant?

TWELVE REASONS SMART ORGANIZATIONS THRIVE IN *ANY* ECONOMY

ROSS SHAFER

Dedication

This book is dedicated to our two-year-old daughter, Lauren Rae Shafer. Every day she reminds us how important it is to stay relevant. She is already nimble with a mouse and a desktop computer, and when I can't find her shoes, she says, "Why don't you Google them, Daddy?" She can deftly negotiate kisses for less naptime. And, she recently taught my wife and me how to properly use chopsticks.

To say that children learn faster and adapt better to change than adults do is grossly understating the obvious.

By the time Lauren enters the workplace, she will most likely be equipped to apply for one of the "top-ten" jobs—jobs that have not even been invented yet!

Special Thanks

First of all, I need to thank Matthew Dale, who started this project with me. Matt is resourceful and an award winning high school psychology teacher and basketball coach at Canyon High School in Anaheim Hills, California. Matt constantly challenged me to open the windows of relevant media and technology. His research and energy for innovative practices were always a thrill for me.

I also need to thank Keri Viere and Stephanie Philips, who transcribed the numerous interviews contained in this book. My handwriting is abominable, yet they fervently deciphered my tapes and unintelligible "scratchings" to find the words of experience held captive within.

I am indebted to the remarkable professionals who gave so freely of their time and expertise. Their perspective gave each chapter its real-life context and a teachable case study. They are Roger Staubach, Jim Sharp, Bruce Nordstrom, Daniel Pink, Jim Collins, Jack Welch, Bob Walsh, Mark McComb, Jim Margraff, Jeffery Munks, Pete Winemiller, Drew Hedgcock, Jeff Stegenga, Richard A. Howard, Richard Schelp, Rich Gibbons, Dornett Wright, Joan Orseck, John Gilpin, Cam Marston, Darrell Zahorsky, Rieva Lesonsky, Steve and Shannon Sorenson, Kevin Webb, Ivar Chinna, Jay Deutsch, Eric Bensussen, Tim Sexton, Rand Rosenberg, Bryant Evan, Lee Dale, Mark Pacinda, Ira Bryck, Steven Rossi, Steve Birdsall, Judith Hess, John Saccheri, and Dr. Norman Stolzoff. You've given me more fun and insight than you know.

Finally, I need to thank my loving family. Thank you to my wife Leah; my two sons, Adam Shafer and Ryan Shafer; and our daughter Lauren (Lolo). All of you inspire me to stay curious and keep learning, and have encouraged me to tattle on the adventures of people much smarter than I am.

Contents

Introduction

Your expertise is expiring!

Is that some sort of author's scare tactic to get your attention?

I hope so.

Believe this: The speed at which your expertise deteriorates ... *is accelerating.*

Precisely because you are successful now means that complacency is creeping in. Don't kid yourself. Your lower-level competitors are in the corner doing one-armed push-ups, waiting for you to get sloppy. They want you to die.

People and organizations that constantly battle complacency are brave enough to test themselves against one survival question: "Are we still relevant?" They lose sleep worrying whether or not they still matter to their shareholders, customers, client, patients, and their employees.

The people and organizations in this book realize that the so-called *wow* factor isn't enough anymore. They know that with sustained growth comes the *now* factor. They accept that best practices are a moving target.

How do I know this?

Every year, I have an all-access backstage pass to nearly one hundred of the most innovative all-company meetings in the world. I spend time in close quarters with the C-Suite—as well as with the rank and file. I am allowed to compare top-tier management missions with the actual line-level execution. I even get hired to tweak their evolving best practices.

This book is the by-product of personal interviews and case studies from the people and companies who *get it*. And they get it in *any* economy. In fact, the best ones refuse to participate in economic downturns. Relevant companies keep growing, even in a stagnant market. But most organizations won't do the work it takes to remain relevant; especially when money gets tight.

You'll find that what these people and companies have to say in this book is actionable and candid, and will absolutely convince you that revenue and profits are inextricably tied to remaining relevant. If you ignore their advice, your market share will be vulnerable to attack.

Still think that opening line was a scare tactic?

Good. Now your adrenalin has kicked in.

Chapter One

Best Practices Are a Moving Target

Great to Good?

First of all, you have to accept that your best practices have an expiration date.

A few months ago, I spent a little time with Jim Collins, best-selling author of *Good to Great*. He talked about the reasons why seven out of the original eleven companies profiled in his book are now not-so-great, judging by relative stock-price slippage and management turnover. Jim said, "We did exhaustive, deep-dive research with these companies. We really thought they were bulletproof. Best management. Best company focus. Best expertise within their market niche. But the great lesson here is ... if a downslide can happen to them, it can happen to anybody."

Jim felt that at least two critical factors caused the declines:

1

1. "These organizations didn't adjust their operational methods to keep pace with new technology. They hung on to their core mission, which was smart, but they didn't adapt to changing operational methods in the market."

2. "These organizations lost their humility. Many of them thought they were too smart to be vulnerable. Many expanded by unsound acquisitions—and if you think there is a war for good talent, there is even a greater war for good companies. There aren't that many out there."

You Should Worry About Your Eventual Extinction

Your company could fold.

Every day we read about famous companies that have had to file for Chapter 11 bankruptcy protection: companies like Bombay Company, CompUSA, The Sharper Image, Musicland, Toys-R-Us, Hollywood Video, Pagenet, Aloha Airlines, ATA Airlines, Woolworths, and so on. Nobody is immune.

How is it that companies can get to Chapter 11 restructuring—or worse, to Chapter 7? (Chapter 7 is the "OK, we give up" stage when the board or the bank decides there is no other option except to shut the whole thing down.)

They've lost their relevance. They've lost their talented leadership. They went spend-crazy and/or acquisition-happy, and are carrying too much debt. Maybe their leases expired or their operations got sloppy. Or they failed to evolve with their industry.

To avoid extinction, your company has to continually ask these questions: "do we have a reason to exist?" And, "would the world miss us if we closed up shop?"

Jeff Stegenga is a professional who is hired to pose those difficult questions to ailing companies. Sadly, things have gotten pretty bad before Stegenga shows up. "Seriously, I'm the guy you don't want to see leaning on your water cooler," he says.

Stegenga is a managing director for Alvarez & Marsal (A&M). A&M is a multinational corporate financing company that provides acquisition counseling and financing, and can offer transition guidance to companies that file Chapter 11. A&M helps companies navigate the waters of restructuring and reorganization.

Stegenga has seen some famous companies teeter on the edge of extinction.

"If you are U.S. Airways, you have to wonder if your viability is wavering because America doesn't need another airline flying similar routes. They've now merged with America West to see if they can use their combined strengths to form one viable airline. The jury is still out," he says.

Stegenga cites Fretter, Inc., based in Detroit, Michigan, and opened in 1951. "At one time, Fretter was a powerhouse in the appliance business. But then along came the much bigger—and identity-driven—Best Buy and Circuit City. Even with the acquisition of established appliance retailers, such as Fred Smid of Colorado, Silo, and YES store, and sales over $540 million, Fretter had to seek bankruptcy protection because they just couldn't adjust to the larger box stores."

According to another analyst, Fretter's problem was that it did not offer a brand differentiator. Asking to remain nameless, he commented, "Fretter was vanilla. You have to stand for something. They were so price-conscious that they never even thought about a personality. You can't just live on price alone, or you'll go out of business."

Dwindling market share, lingering debt from the acquisitions, and an outdated store format eventually doomed Fretter to failure in 1996.

Stegenga is also close to the Movie Gallery Company, whose retail brand is Hollywood Video. Movie Gallery recently filed Chapter 11 because they didn't respond well when the movie rental business evolved to embrace Internet models, such as

Netflix and Blockbuster. Stegenga points out that "the movie business has changed. When I take my eight-year-old son to a multiplex, we look around and see five or six people in the entire theater, and we wonder how they can keep the lights on with such a small audience."

Other times, changing consumer demands can shift an entire national habit and render a company irrelevant. After President Bill Clinton gave a ringing endorsement to Krispy Kreme doughnuts, the country rushed to their doors. The long lines were worth the wait. Watching hundreds of fresh doughnuts baked and slathered with icing right before your eyes made the premium price seem like a bargain.

That is, until Dr. Robert Atkins taught America how to eat fewer carbohydrates and eliminate junk foods. Krispy Kreme, who was in the midst of expanding exponentially, became an instant casualty of the Atkins philosophy. In May 2004, the company issued a profit warning, saying diets such as Atkins and South Beach had hit them hard. Stock shares fell 29 percent in one day. Once reaching a high of $48 per share in late 2003, Krispy Kreme (KKD) now resides in the $4-per-share range.

In 2003, the Atkins diet took a fatal hit when its founder, Dr. Robert Atkins, died. After his demise, America apparently fell out of love with Atkins Nutritionals; about two years later, the company filed for Chapter 11 bankruptcy protection.

Several factors contributed to the Atkins phenomenon's descent into irrelevancy. The company overspent on marketing to vie with competitors that had been in the food business for a hundred years. Atkins also got too cocky about the value of their brand and started charging triple the prices for energy bars, supplements, and other food products—not a good strategy when consumers have a choice. Finally, Kraft Foods, Unilever, and General Mills all jumped on the low-carbohydrate bandwagon, and they had more resources and a far better selection of tasty products.

After struggling for a few years, Atkins reemerged in 2006 as a licensed brand for related food products. You could say they are searching for renewed relevance, albeit under the radar.

You Mean To Tell Me
Kodak Didn't See This Coming?

Even the best brands in the world are susceptible to danger.

I was at a Kodak meeting in the late '90s when a top sales executive stood up and arrogantly told the group, "Don't be freaked out by this digital photography thing. It's only a fad for early adopters." Dismissing that kind of innovation caused Kodak's stock to drop from $87 per share in 1997 to $14 per share in summer 2008. Living in denial of their irrelevance has hurt their employee recruiting campaign and their market share. Polaroid (which is now an over-the-counter stock) exhibited similar denial toward the digital revolution. Perhaps Polaroid thought people waving their pictures in the air to dry and develop was a better business model.

Reinvent Yourself — Or Die

Remaining relevant is your best survival tactic. Relevant companies continue to grow in any economy, even in a finite or stagnant market.

Why? Because most organizations stupidly refuse to do the work it takes to keep reinventing themselves. Complacency will render your market share vulnerable to attack. If there was one inoculation a company should get, it would be a vaccination to guard against the disease of complacency. Complacency can lull a once-successful organization into collecting easy profits on old products or services and not seeking innovation to stay important.

The second most dangerous corporate affliction is suppressing viable growth ideas. Too many times individual egos override team goals.

The best executives will not tolerate this. I witnessed Jack Welch tell a group of respected telecom executives that when he ran General Electric, he would severely punish a manager for not sharing his or her best practices. That policy became an inside joke at G.E.

"Did you hear about the manager who called Jack's office and told his assistant, 'Hey, I think we're onto something really cool here in Des Moines. Please tell Jack immediately so I don't get caught with it.'"

Relevant people actively share ideas and information to keep their edge. Irrelevant people hoard best practices in a selfish effort to temporarily give their department an edge. If you work for a hoarder, quit today. You are a passenger on a sinking ship.

Relevant Review

Your famous brand doesn't insure long-term success. It only makes your fall from grace more public. Smaller, more nimble companies will always try to steal your customers and your market share. They will succeed if you become complacent about your "dominance" and are unaware that best practices are constantly evolving.

Aggressive organizations know that remaining relevant means consciously acknowledging that today's expertise may not work tomorrow. They have the courage to ask scary questions:

- "Has our business model changed?"
- "Have the reliable and profitable paradigms of our industry shifted?"
- "Is our competition starting to gobble up our market share? If so, how did that happen?"
- "How can we hire and retain the best talent?"

- "What kind of employee incentives should we offer?"
- "How can we compete against the global giants?"
- "What kind of market research should we be doing?"
- "Should we still have a training department?"
- "How much (and what kind of) technology do we need?"
- "How do our competitors keep innovating?"
- "Should we be more socially responsible? If so, how?"

If You Are Not Relevant, How Do You Get There Fast?

Today's consumers—as well as business-to-business customers—are demanding and savvy. They expect you to be more current than they are. They are willing to offer loyalty, but they're also quick to identify inauthentic organizations. So, be genuine. The smartest organizations don't fake relevance.

They constantly police it.

Chapter 2

There Is No Recession
When You Innovate

Just in case you don't finish this book (and I can't imagine why you wouldn't), you *have* to read this chapter. This chapter alone will spark your thinking on remaining on the relevant edge. It might even be the most important chapter in the book. (How's that for a tease?)

Every aggressive organization with which I've ever worked wants to be bigger. They want more market share; they want the best people working for them. Oh, and they want a feature story in the *Wall Street Journal*.

There at least five ways to make that happen. The first four won't surprise you. The fifth is the gold mine. Innovation is the most accessible and affordable growth driver for any size business. (Speed readers may skip to #5.)

1. Grow organically by maximizing internal processes and paying attention to your customers on an emotional basis. They will keep coming back out of loyalty. They will tell two friends ... who tell two friends ... and so on. Growth can be exponential with this method.

2. Buy another business. Acquire other companies who complement your market base. This is tricky: if you think there's a talent shortage, you're really going to find a *talented company* shortage. There just aren't that many good companies to buy. Jack Welch told me that he tried to buy a new company every ten days, and they had a huge staff working on it. It was so difficult that they had to buy a mortgage banking company to help them—and that company nearly went bankrupt after the acquisition.

3. Go global. If you think you can play on the global stage, you could start exporting your goods and services internationally. However, this is a dangerous way to grow, unless you have trusted partners overseas who can help you navigate the distance and the cultural differences.

4. Franchise. Package your goods or services in such a way that they can be successful anywhere and you've got a scalable franchise opportunity.

5. Innovation. This is the growth secret that can cause your organization to sprint ahead of your competition—regardless of your size. This method will *always* be relevant. Come up with something entirely new. Invent a new way of operating your business. Devise a new product or service that solves a new or ongoing problem.

The awesome power of innovation argues that size doesn't matter. Who would have thought a couple of Stanford students would ever be able to compete against Microsoft and Yahoo in the search engine business? Larry Page and Sergey Brin, founders of Google, were not intimidated. They had faith in a better idea.

Hundreds of Small Innovations Matter

Darrell Zahorsky is a writer for About.com. He also is a brilliant speaker whose original ideas on the subject of innovation—ideas that can be found at www.profitinnovators.com—are in demand worldwide. His daily job is to create actionable, concise insights for business owners that can move their businesses forward. He sees innovation as the answer to "the next big thing," because big, radical innovations are sexy and newsworthy. As you can imagine, finding and executing such innovations may take years of costly research. The odds of success on those industry-changing shifts are something like one in a thousand. What small business has that kind of time or money for that kind of risk?

Ross Shafer: Big innovations are newsworthy, but you think such big innovations are too rare for most companies?
Darrell Zahorsky: Businesses need to focus on small innovations where the success odds are closer to one in ten. With small innovations, they're very difficult to copy because you could implement a lot of them as opposed to one big idea. Everybody can copy a big idea, but if you have hundreds and hundreds of small innovations, that's like your secret recipe. Nobody's going to be able to copy that as readily. Besides, a lot of those innovations will be internal—things that your competitors can't see.
RS: If I'm looking for small innovations, where will I find them?
DZ: Small innovations can come from anywhere in the organization: a clerk, a bellman, a secretary. That's where small innovations gestate. They are often something so simple or mundane that most people overlook them. But the impacts can produce huge profits. I think a good example of that was in '98, when a couple of Stanford Web guys—Larry Page and Sergey Brin—were doing some codes for a search engine. They had no HTML experience, so they just put up a blank and very simple home page, and that became Google.

Part of their success was that they didn't overthink the solution—
they just eliminated the clutter on their home page. That gave them
faster download times, and people just loved the fact that it was so
simple. When they had that idea, it was just something that they
needed to get done. There was nothing complex or radical with
that innovation, but the simple became a very big idea—a great example of a cool but small innovation.

The Lush Innovation

Lush is a $100-million-a-year cosmetics company. They sell hand-
made bath products, soaps, and lotions in thirty-five countries. What
makes them so relevant to their customers is that they look to their
customers for innovation. Lush Cosmetics doesn't just have a blog.
They have an interactive forum. Customers can post their messages
on the Lush site and get a quick response back from the company.
These customers, or "Lushies," as they're called, have a voice in product development. Lushies have actually created quite a number of
successful new products for the company. Literally tens of thousands
of customers participate in the online forums.

While a lot of bigger organizations are not willing to listen to
the bad news, Lush is relevant because they use the customers'
feedback—good and bad—to connect with their customers. Lush
isn't so arrogant as to second-guess what their customers really
think is relevant.

How You Can Double Your Dog Business

While I was interviewing Darrell Zahorsky about innovation, he
brought up his wife's dog-sitting business as an example. Angie
Zahorsky has a business called "Happy Hounds by Angie." Already

a dog lover, Angie started offering dog-walking and overnight stays in a very affluent market. But how could she compete when there were already plenty of established dog-sitting businesses?

Innovation.

Many pet sitters offer free consultations. They typically go to owners' homes, present their credentials, whatever licenses they have, insurance, testimonials, and so on. What Angie does is very different. Throughout her free consultation, she focuses her attention entirely on the dog. She still speaks to the owners, but she realizes that ultimately the dog is the customer. If that "customer" is happy, the owner will be happy.

There is something else quite different about Angie's service.

Angie's fee is twice as much as other dog sitters' fees. But her simple change of perspective is so effective that it has created a waiting list for her services.

Angie also has been able to borrow ideas from other industries. She employs a "cross-pollination approach." She has taken ideas from the $3-billion-a-year scrapbooking industry. She has a digital camera, and she takes pictures of various events that happen during the first month of the dog's life in her care. She then puts those photos into a gift scrapbook for her clients.

What small innovations could you launch within your industry?

Wristwatches Are Losing Popularity Everywhere ... But Here

According to recent research, wristwatch sales are sliding down 11 percent a year. We don't need them as much anymore. If you went to any shopping mall and polled a dozen eighteen-year-olds, you would only see a wristwatch on one of them. Why? Because they can get the time by looking at their cell phones or PDAs.

That trend doesn't seem to be affecting The Watch Man store

in Laughlin, Nevada. They sell more wristwatches than any other store in the world—some twenty thousand every year. What might shock you is that the store's location isn't very glamorous. The Watch Man occupies about two thousand square feet inside a small, remote casino.

However, size and glamour don't matter because The Watch Man has employed a clever innovation. They don't lock their watches behind glass cases or tall, plastic kiosk cylinders. They don't believe that the watches will quickly be stolen if they are placed in open view. At The Watch Man, all of the watches are laid out on long, open tables. So the customer thinks, "These people trust me."

If you walked through their wide front door today, you would see thousands of wristwatches exposed and a big sign that reads:

> **Pick It Up. Try It On. If You See One On My Wrist That You Like, Take It Off Me.**

This also is a fun place to visit. The Watch Man's fun starts every morning at 8:50 AM. The store opens at 9:00 AM, but ten minutes before opening, there's always a "Spin for Spirit." All the employees gather around a *Wheel of Fortune*-type wheel, and the managers start chanting, "Watch Man. Watch Man. Rah, rah, rah! Watch Man. Watch Man. Rah, rah, rah! Let's go have fun today! Let's sell a lot of watches today!" The noise is almost deafening—but also very infectious. When you're standing outside the locked gate, you feel as if you're missing out on something fun. Then, when the cheering and applause starts to die down, the floodgates open and customers stream in at full speed.

One of the founders, Mack Jett, told me, "It doesn't matter what business you're in—and we've been in a few—our only job is to create customers. We do that by having fun and keeping in mind that we want lifetime employees, which, in turn, creates lifetime customers."

Notice how Jett said he wanted "lifetime *employees*" before he said "lifetime *customers*"?

He has the order right. One spawns the other.

The Watch Man founders truly care about their employees. Mack Jett and his partner, Ray Lindstrom, innovate fun ideas for growth at every level of the organization. For example, the watch repair technician also doubles as an Elvis impersonator twice a day. The operations manager creates cooking contests, offers personal counseling sessions, and organizes company bowling tournaments. Each hour, employees take turns on the store PA system to spin the "Spirit Wheel" and hand out door prizes to customers. At The Watch Man, clerks don't say, "May I help you?" Instead, they greet you with, "Are you having fun today?"

Their customer care policy? If you buy a watch and it stops working, they will repair or replace it for free. No questions. No arguments.

The experience is fun, but what makes it relevant is that The Watch Man's perspective is always aimed at the customer's point of view. One woman got all the way back to her home in Paris, France, and her watch stopped. The Watch Man sent her three new wristwatches for free.

Innovation Is Often About
Evolution and Refining Perfection

Television is the great cultural barometer.

Having spent a good many years in the television industry hosting and producing talk shows, game shows, news magazines, and so on, I took for granted that TV shows came and went with shifts in cultural dynamics. We had a constant quest to tap into the public's tastes and interests. After the September 11, 2001, attacks on the World Trade Center, survival and testing-your-will shows became popular. The viewers' desire to see real people in action, living out the drama of cohabitating or battling for evasive affections, fueled the reality-TV boom. Watching amateurs argue was more interesting than following a scripted, laugh-track-supported situation comedy, which is why it took so long to settle the hundred-day writer's strike of 2007–2008.

The television industry must remain vigilant to audience moods. If viewers lose interest and stop watching, we know it instantly, courtesy of the national overnight viewer-ratings systems. Sadly, many organizations still rely on quarterly reports because it's easier. But waiting three months to see how you've done is a dangerous game of market arrogance.

Great organizations monitor sales performance daily.

"Jumping the Shark"
Signals the Death of an Irrelevant Brand

Have you ever witnessed the jumping of a shark?

Since the advent of the Internet, television viewers aggressively weigh in about the popularity (and unpopularity) of their favorite TV shows. The Website www.jumptheshark.com tries to pinpoint the exact moment viewers started tuning out.

The term "jump the shark" is derived from the moment viewers thought the TV show *Happy Days* had gone too far astray from its original, accepted characters and storyline. In an eighth-season episode, Henry Winkler's character, Fonzie, jumps over a penned-in shark in a moment of ultimate "cool" while water skiing.

Rabid fans were outraged.

Not only was the premise absurd, they postulated that Fonzie would never go water skiing in the first place. Fans felt betrayed by the show. They thought *Happy Days* had started to veer dramatically away from their core competencies in search of stretched storylines.

Viewers also said Will Smith's *Fresh Prince of Bel-Air* jumped the shark when the same character, Vivian, was suddenly played by a different actress—and nobody said anything about the switch!

And on the *Facts of Life,* a sitcom about four teenage girls, one viewer thought the shark got jumped on the episode where Natalie, played by Mindy Cohen, lost her virginity. Says a fan, "They should have kept Natalie and the other gals fresh, at least until they got married. This is a show aimed at girls, so what message was this sending out?"

To give you an idea of how the viewers' pulse is read in this industry, I turned to Jim Sharp, Senior Vice President of Original Programming and Development for the Comedy Central TV Network.

Ross Shafer: You and I created a TV show that stayed on the air for sixteen seasons—*Almost Live*—with full knowledge that all television shows are eventually terminal. Every show eventually goes off the air. You've had success with two comedy shows that have been on the air a long time: *The Daily Show with Jon Stewart* and *South Park.* The only reason they exist today is that they must be relevant. Your continued success has to be because your shows continue to be relevant to their audience.

Jim Sharp: Yeah, there's no question that those two shows have been successful. I mean, *The Daily Show* continues to just grow and grow, and every time you pick up a survey, we see more and more people actually get their hard news from *The Daily Show.* Those statistics give us an indication about where younger people get their news.

RS: And how do you think that happened? It's still a comedy show.

JS: It's still a comedy show, yeah. I just think it grew over time, and they're just on top of their game ... relevant by nature.

RS: And the guest lineup keeps getting better. That's a good indicator of relevance.

JS: Right. It amazes me who will appear on that show. President Clinton to—well, you name the hot celebrity. People will consent to being a guest on that show because they reach a very young, important audience: those eighteen- to forty-nine-year-olds. And, I have to emphasize, it's funny first, but it's also as topical as it can be. It's produced on the same "day and date" it is aired. You get to hear what the culture is thinking about on that day. You can get your news, you can get your information, and you can get a different comic take.

RS: Was that show originally born as that "brand," or did it develop?

JS: It developed into what it is today to stay relevant. The first host was Craig Kilborn, if you remember. And I was there when the show launched in 1997. And I remember Doug Herzog, who was the president [of MTV Entertainment Networks] then, and is now on his second term. He was determined to launch a show that was like what *SportsCenter* is to sports, but this show would be geared to comedy, news, and politics. While it certainly has evolved over the years, the core hasn't changed. It's got a solid format. It's had two really good hosts. I mean, I think you'll agree Jon clearly has taken it to a different level.

RS: Yeah, Jon is a cable host who has become a giant mainstream star, even hosting the world's most popular television broadcast, the Oscars.

JS: And his show is really an extension of him and his sensibilities toward comedy. The correspondents that have gone through there have become known personalities. It's kind of like the new farm team for comedians. I mean, look at people like Stephen Colbert and Steve Carell and Lewis Black.

RS: They've all gone on to bigger careers from their exposure on *The Daily Show.*

JS: And even though they have moved on, the show's ratings and content just keep getting better and better. By its nature, it is a TV show that must remain relevant to continue to reflect the audience's tastes and interests. They covered the 2004 presidential election, which is always a big year for a political show because covering the presidential campaigns and debates provides fuel for great comedy. So you would expect to get a viewer-ratings spike there. We all thought the ratings would come back down to earth after the election was over. Well, that didn't happen. What happened was that more people were exposed to *The Daily Show*. They liked it, thought it was funny, thought it was relevant, thought it was important, and so they continued to watch. Now, in 2008, the numbers are the highest they've ever been.

RS: OK. Let's talk about *South Park* because that's been a staple on your network for a very long time. I am usually not a fan of cartoon shows because they seem to revisit the same joke over and over. But *South Park*'s topicality makes it unpredictable in that way. Do you think, similar to *The Simpsons*, *South Park* continues to rage on for that reason?

JS: Yeah. I mean, look, those guys [producers Trey Parker and Matt Stone] are just so smart, and I think they did their best work last year. It just keeps getting better and better. It's almost like the old *Saturday Night Live* days: when something bizarre happens in the news, like Tom Cruise and his Scientology controversy, you can't wait to see what the kids in *South Park* are going to say about it.

RS: Do you get a heads-up about what they are going to cover in any given week?

JS: I never know what they're going to do. They write and direct that show week to week. They see something interesting in the news and get it on the air somehow. It has that topicality to it, too. Certainly not the immediacy of same day and date like *The Daily Show,* but if something newsworthy happens in the culture, you can look forward to getting their take on it.

RS: Like any successful TV show, they have carefully developed distinctly unique characters that sustain over time.

JS: Yes. *South Park* has these four outrageous kids on the show; so it's not so much a dysfunctional family like *The Simpsons.*

RS: But since the kids never age and the culture is always providing fresh material, it's a formula that could go twenty years—like *The Simpsons.*

JS: I hope you're right.

RS: Let's talk about the Comedy Central brand. You have stayed pretty strict to your brand: if it isn't funny, it won't appear on your network. Is that philosophy easier for you than other networks?

JS: We're all about our brand, and yes, our brand is a little bit narrower. But we're also a growth company. If part of the charge is to grow, then I think we have to broaden our market a little bit, and I think we're trying to figure out how to do that. But we will do it carefully. I think as any company broadens out, you run the risk of breaking your brand promise to your "customers," and maybe even disappointing some people. I think people tune in to Comedy Central and expect to see a certain kind of comedy that they won't see elsewhere.

RS: Right.

JS: We often say that if something can live on another network, it probably will not work on Comedy Central.

RS: You also are fond of saying, "Anything we do has to have a reason to live here." Actually, that philosophy applies to every product or service in any business. We should all be very intentional about identifying and executing our unique advantages.

JS: Absolutely. And when we define our specific advantage, we use all those adjectives like "irreverent," "edgy," or "risky," but it's true. We try to be all those things as long as we stay funny first.

RS: Can you give us an example of something normally outside the bandwidth of Comedy Central that turned out to be a brand risk worth taking?

JS: The best example of that, Ross, is the Blue Collar Comedy stuff. The Blue Collar stuff always works here. Someone could argue that Blue Collar Comedy isn't hip or edgy enough. But an audience always finds it, every single time. We run the Blue Collar movies and the numbers go through the roof every time they air. And all four of those talented comedians [Jeff Foxworthy, Bill Engvall, Larry the Cable Guy, Ron White] have had half-hour stand-up specials here. So clearly there's room to be a little bit broader and expand that brand—as long as it's funny first, and it's accessible to our audience.

RS: Can you define what you mean by "accessible"?

JS: [*laughs*] I just heard it in a meeting once and it sounded smart, so I try to slip it in from time to time. Seriously, it means the audience can relate to the humor and likes it enough to stay tuned. See, now I don't sound so smart, do I?

RS: You're the smartest person in this room. On another subject, *The Colbert Report,* starring Stephen Colbert, is doing great as well.

JS: It's a hit. It's an example of testing a concept with an audience on *The Daily Show* and rolling it out as a series.

RS: That show looks like it's been on the air for years.

JS: It came out of the blocks and they were up to speed instantly. The show immediately looked great. It was smart and funny, and Stephen was just so ready for that after having all those years of experience on *The Daily Show.* He took the persona that he developed there and ran with it.

RS: I thought he was a great segment on *The Daily Show*, but I wondered if that character was big enough to sustain a whole show.

JS: And now we know the answer is yes.

RS: The people who already liked him got exactly what they expected, so there weren't any surprises like, "Oh, now the guy's wearing sweaters" or "Now he's going to be doing license-plate-logo humor," or that kind of thing.

JS: No, no, he's really stayed true to his character, and I think that's the key. It just really worked. But, you know, both *The Daily Show* and *The Colbert Report* are comedy shows first. But, in fact, people tune in to those shows to find out what's going on in the world or what's going on in news in general. It's been kind of interesting.

RS: Do they have a strong blog, forum, or Internet presence?

JS: Yeah, they both do, especially *The Colbert Report.* It's called Colbert Nation, and the producers have made that a priority.

Their website is huge, too. The audience for those shows is loyal and participatory. More importantly, they keep showing up to watch. That's the true test of relevance, if people keep showing up to buy what you're selling.

Can a Dying Sport Like Bowling Be Innovative?

I used to go bowling as a kid because everyone in our neighborhood did. All the moms I knew were in a Tuesday-night league. My mom and her friends wore identical silk shirts, and it was cool.

But in the past twenty years, traditional bowling-lane operators have watched league play dwindle from six nights a week to one night a week—if that. Couples in which both partners work full time simply can't commit to that kind of time. And if they do have a free night, they have a lot of other choices. Some bowling owners have been forced to abandon league bowling altogether. They are trying to attract bowlers with gimmicks like Cosmic Bowling (black lights & lasers), 99-cent-lane nights, video-game rooms, and "bumper bowling." Bumper bowling uses a fence-like device that actually pops up and blocks the ball from going into the gutters. That way, youngsters can learn to roll the ball—and hit the pins—without dumping all those gutter balls. We have a young daughter, so I really like this innovation.

However, the most outrageous, next-generation, bowling-lane chain has listened to what caused this cultural icon to erode, and has provided an alternative.

As we go to print, Lucky Strike Lanes has eleven locations and is changing the entire bowling-alley experience. They promote themselves as "America's First Bowling Lounge." Each location boasts a forty-feet-high exterior wall mural of a sexy woman caressing a bowling ball. The front entrance looks more like a nightclub than a bowling alley. Inside, the look is also, well ... uh ... sexy. There is a trendy looking sports bar area with plasma TVs. Off to one side is a private, four-lane bowling area set up for parties. The main lanes are outfitted with large, comfy lounge chairs and couches instead of the old, hard, fiberglass bucket seats. The scoreboard is a forty-two-inch plasma monitor that automatically calculates all the scores for you. No more broken pencils and tough tenth-frame arithmetic. The projection-screen walls behind the pins display sports-bar-friendly images. After 10:00 PM, the artwork changes to reflect a more adult mood. It's *Sex and the City* goes bowling.

And, the food is great.

The first tip-off is that Lucky Strike doesn't sell nachos with the liquid-cheese option. In fact, they've hired real chefs at each location.

Do they make money?

Compare this: while some lane operators are scrambling to fill their 99-cent-lane nights, Lucky Strike Lanes might rent out the whole club for $40,000 a night. Corporations and publicity companies are using Lucky Strike Lanes for everything from wedding receptions to movie premieres.

When a cultural shift takes place within your customer base (i.e., their interests and habits change), only fools live in denial.

Innovators profit by remaining relevant.

Innovate By Hiring Older Workers!

Here's an innovative idea. Hire experienced people!

Many companies have let talented people go to make room for less expensive, younger workers. Oftentimes they cull the herd by offering "golden parachute" retirement packages to extremely talented older people, only to rehire them as valuable consultants.

Northrop Grumman (NG), the company responsible for some of the most sophisticated aircraft used in combat around the world, is hiring back experience and talent. I spoke with John Gilpin, president of NG's Material Management group. Gilpin is in charge of many products in the fighter-plane group. In fact, the latest fighter plane, the F-35, will replace the current, state-of-the-art F-18. This next-generation fighter jet will have "Harrier" capabilities—meaning it can take off straight up—and will still be able to achieve supersonic airspeeds of 770+ mph. Gilpin was charged with putting together the best minds in the business to build this plane. His considerable experience taught him where to find those minds.

Ross Shafer: John, you've got quite a menu of warplanes on your plate.

John Gilpin: Yeah. I've got a little bit of B-2 bomber. I've got the new F-35. I've got the F-5, T-38, and a little bit of the Global Hawk. So I've got a little bit of everything.

RS: First, let me ask you about the significance of this new F-35. It is obviously a hot issue and very exciting. It is, without question, the most impressive new fighter jet in years. What did that do for your team when that award came in?

JG: It was very energizing, and confirmed that our company has the best team for the job. It's very exciting to get a program like that because it's next-generation. I don't know if you know how that whole thing came together, but a lot of countries have invested in the program, and quite a few—all those different—the Marines, the Navy, the Air Force—have all invested in it. And, as customers, they've put their specific requirements into it. This airplane does several things. For one, it takes off vertically from the aircraft carrier, like a Harrier does. So in the future, this plane is going to take the place of several planes, as far as capabilities.

RS: I've talked to several Navy admirals who say it's a brilliant warplane because they also can put it on smaller watercraft, so they can get their ships in closer to where they need to be.

JG: They wanted that kind of flexibility so that they didn't have to restrict fighter fleets only to large aircraft carriers.

RS: And, as I recall, the F-35 was something like a $200 billion order?

JG: That's huge. We're really excited about winning the award.

RS: A project like this puts a lot of people to work. But they have to be talented, strong, state-of-the-art people. You've done something quite unique when it comes to hiring.

JG: Right. I went out and solicited people who I know have worked in the business before. I tracked down folks who worked at Northrop before, or worked on the B-2 program before, or worked on other programs but left our company and went to other companies.

RS: Experienced folks you could count on to hit the ground running?

JG: Yes. I talked to a lot of the best folks. I said, "Hey, do you know anybody who's still out there who's got aircraft experience that we should draw on to beef up?" I want to get people who come highly recommended, who have the experience and the job knowledge, and who can pretty much just come on board and fit right in—get going right away. I needed top-quality people.

RS: Was it important for them to know or be aware of the Northrop culture?

JG: Oh, yeah. I think our name stands for itself and the heritage that we have. A lot of these guys are just thrilled to be here. Many said, "Oh, yeah. I'll drop this job and come back." Northrop has done a very good job attracting employees because we continue to look at the job market and look at the other companies to see what they're making. We're making exciting products here—history-making aircraft. We can make competitive adjustments as far as wages. And another thing: we make sure that employees are very happy with what we give them as far as benefits and wages. So happy, in fact, that they don't need a union. We are very proud of that.

Can You "Innovate" a Dental Office?

Teeth are teeth, right? They've been in the same places in our mouths forever. Nothing new about the location of our teeth. No surprises there. Outside of whitening technology, porcelain veneers, and orthodontics, what could be considered "innovative" in the world of tooth care?

How about changing the way you run the office? One organization has revamped the entire dental community with a structure that could very well be the future of other professional healthcare organizations. I interviewed two of the partners of Gentle Dental, Kevin Webb and Ivar Chinna.

Ross Shafer: You have been very innovative in redefining the dental office. You have exploded to 130 offices in eight states. You operate as a large and innovative dental group. Explain how this works as a business and as a benefit for the dental patient.

Kevin Webb: Sure. We have a dental corporation that employs all of the doctors, and there is a management company that employs the rest of the staff in an office, and the nonclinical staff. The doctors just practice dentistry. They don't manage the business. Think of it this way: Gentle Dental is a dental-management company that hires dentists to perform dentistry. So for our intents and purposes, the management company does everything except get their hands wet in a patient's mouth. I know that sounds kind of graphic, but that's about the best way I can describe it to you. And what we also do is try to provide a lot of continuing education and training to our dentists. Why? Because a lot of our dentists, for whatever reason, did not enjoy being in private practice on their own. A lot of our dentists have come out of the largest group practice in the world: the U.S. military. And so we really function as a large group practice. From a functional, day-to-day basis, there's no difference between the professional dental corporation and the management company in terms of how everything works in an office. A patient never sees anything separate.

Ivar Chinna: I try to relate our business to a mom and dad. In a really good family unit, the same question is asked of a mom or dad. Individually, you get the same answer, and that's kind of the way we try to work with our organization. From Oklahoma City; or Honolulu, Hawaii; or McMinnville, Oregon; or Everett, Washington—spread out among eight states, we have 130 locations, and they're part of one big group.

RS: And within the group, you offer more than general dentistry, correct?

IC: Yes. If you need to see an oral surgeon, an orthodontist, an endodontist, a periodontist, a pediatric dentist, or whatever specialty, most of our offices provide that care in addition to the general dentist. The model that we're striving for is really customer-focused for all of the customer's needs.

RS: It is refreshing to hear you refer to patients as customers, because that's exactly who they are ... and how they think of themselves ... and how they relate their experiences with you.

KW: We know dentistry can be difficult for people, especially if you find out that you need to see a specialist. Let's say your regular dentist is Dr. Aaron, and Dr. Aaron needs to refer you to a specialist. Instead of driving across town or wherever that specialist may be, our business model is to have you come back to that same office. Built into that model is the ability for your dentist to be able to communicate about you, as a patient, to one of the seven specialists who also practice in the same office. We really try to make sure you have the best overall care.

IC: From a patient's perspective, you don't have to get referred to somebody who may or may not accept your insurance—or to someone you don't know. Instead, you'd be walking right down the hall to talk about your care. In fact, doing your full care together and doing a consultation together is all possible in our office. It's a really great, patient-centric model.

RS: How do the doctors like it?

IC: It's good for doctors, too. By being in that group practice that Kevin described, it's a much comfier, friendlier place than being out on your own in a solo practice where you have to learn from yourself. Typically, you get out of school and you're in debt from your school loans, and you're further in debt from opening up a practice and hoping patients come in the door. And you don't have anybody really to learn from but yourself. With us, you can come into our warm, comfy environment, and we have a whole bunch of patients ready to go. We have a lot of senior people all around you to teach you how to get acclimated to the business and improve your professional skills. And we have the flexibility that goes with being a large group practice. You can work different hours—you can move to a different state if you want to—and still have a place to hang your hat and build a practice. And so there's a whole bunch of reasons to join us, from the dentist side, as well, so we think we've hit both sides of the equation with our model.

RS: I like this model because you have the opportunity to manage all of the customer empathy touch points, from the first moment with a general practitioner to whomever the customer is referred to downstream.

KW: Precisely. If I do a great job and then send you off to somebody on the other side of town, I can't guarantee that you're going to get the great experience you had with me, which would certainly reflect on me and my business.

RS: This way you can maintain consistent patient empathy from start to finish.

KW: I think talking about how, as you call it, "empathy touch points"—or our ability to make sure that, as a group practice, we're working together, we're consistently representing the same image to our patients—is really important.

RS: I've seen quite a few health-care organizations, but I've never seen one take such a wall-to-wall patient approach like this.

IC: What's probably different about us from other health-care operations is that, traditionally, health care hasn't been service-oriented. We have the flavor of a more retail-oriented, service-oriented version of health care than you've probably seen or dealt with in the past. We've tried to take the entire business model and flip it on its ears, so that it's not the benefits that matter; it's the patient who matters.

RS: Even your hours of operation are different.

IC: We all—including the dentists—are there to serve the patients, and to that end, we're going to be open mornings, nights, weekends, or whenever patients want appointments. We're going to have full-service care available—including specialty care—and as many offices as we can. We take all forms of insurance. We're conveniently located and not stuck off in some medical building that's hard to find and hard to park near. So it's better all around.

Relevant Review

Steal ideas from the best companies.

You will learn invaluable lessons from the people and organizations in this book. And don't you dare dismiss them just because they are not in your industry. In fact, be thankful that they aren't competing against you. Instead, steal their ideas and inspirations. Cross-pollinate their genius into your field ... *before your competition does.*

Whether you are a bowling alley, a fighter-jet manufacturer, a television network, a watch store, or a dental office, innovation is the secret weapon your competition can never see coming. Innovation doesn't have to be big. It doesn't have to be costly. And, you don't have the pressure to devise "the next big thing" breakthrough. Dozens of small innovations can cause a massive tidal shift in your industry that could catapult you into the market-leader position. When "intentional innovation" is a part of your regular business diet, you'll have purchased the cheapest insurance policy intelligence can buy. Put another way, innovation is the core catalyst for relevance.

Do a forensic examination of your organization. What could you do to revolutionize your production process? Your inventory procedure? Your service menu and warranty models? Your incentive structure? Your hiring practices? What could you do to maximize your human resources? If you were a new customer or client, what would you *really* want from you that nobody else is providing?

Everything you do is worth improving.

Chapter 3

The Sneaky Ways Your Competition Steals the Best Talent

Winning the Talent War Isn't That Complicated

The talent war is real.

You already know how hard it is to find great people, or you wouldn't care about reading this chapter. Furthermore, the most sought-after employees are savvy these days. They've learned there is such a thing as "the employer of choice." So naturally, the best people want to work "there."

Here is your other challenge. Since a large segment of the baby-boomer workforce is retiring, how will you find and keep *young* talent that can take your organization to the elusive next level? Will you have to offer more incentive packages? A company gym? A subsidized lunchroom?

Shockingly, no.

They primarily want to feel important and useful.

Boomers, Move Over

Not to insult you baby boomers, but unless you get relevant fast, you are going to be replaced sooner than you want to be. The younger X and Y generations are more relevant than you are. To define the groups by age, the Xers were born between 1960 and 1979, and Generation Y (aka Millennials or Mils) were born between 1980 and 1999.

These generations love change. Think about how excited they got when a new software version was announced. Or how anxious they were to bootleg a new video-game upgrade. They grew up knowing that *beta* versions were a cutting-edge improvement. They always looked at change as something better. They instinctively knew that nobody changes to be ... worse.

By the way, they will be running your company in ten to fifteen years. Don't make them adapt to your ways. Learn how to adapt to theirs if you want to remain relevant.

Millennials: Why Do You Need Them?

So much has been written about our new—and most numerous—workforce: men and women born after 1980. At 82 million strong, they will shape our futures and take over our industries. Stop complaining about how different they are from you. They will be in charge whether you like it or not. And that's a good thing. Look at their strengths: they are confident, tech savvy, and highly qualified, and are ready to contribute, succeed, and thrive in the ever-changing, ever-growing, and technologically booming business world.

But You Don't Understand Millennials?

If you're a boomer or an Xer, here are some clues.

Millennials define contribution, success, and thriving in much different terms than did previous generations. They value life balance over a sixty-five-hour workweek. They grew up looking forward to video-game code breakers and software updates. Therefore, they embrace change as an improvement, not as a threat. They will not take the highest-paying position just for more money. They want to feel good about the job they do and how it honors the rest of the world. That is why they are so interested in the environment and social issues. While boomers are heralded for their unsinkable work ethic, Millennials want to achieve on their own schedules.

Put aside your differences in ideologies. Instead, aggressively seek the highly resourceful talents the Millennials have to offer.

To learn more about this complex and invaluable workforce, I interviewed Cam Marston. Marston is a highly sought-after speaker/consultant, and author of *Motivating the "What's in it for Me?" Workforce.*

Ross Shafer: Cam, you do a ton of speaking and writing on the subject of generational insights in the workforce. How can boomers be relevant to the younger workforce, the Millennials?

Cam Marston: Defining relevance is quite different between the generations. Boomers gauge relevancy on being facile, based on what they've learned. They like being good at doing the same thing. They have mastered the process. They repeat the process, and, in their minds, that keeps them relevant. The Millennials—people born after 1980—define relevancy as "knowing what's going on" in many different areas of their business and their job, and keeping an open and flexible mind as to what it takes to get the job done.

RS: Considering the vastly different perspectives, where are the management challenges?

CM: That's where I see a lot of the management challenges. A boomer manager may say, "We've done it this way for twenty years. We don't need to change because it's a proven method." And because they have a history of successfully doing their jobs the same way, they get the contentment of getting results. They consider that relevant. But the younger workers are saying, "The more change I can interpret and experience that relates to my workplace, the more relevant I can be." It is almost a conflict of ideology as to what *relevant* truly means.

RS: Why do you think the Millennials have come to think this way?

CM: The world has become so much smaller, particularly with the Internet, technology— even the way that news is reported. Life— and everything in it—seems to happen much more quickly, and they feel that it has an impact on them personally. That may sound a bit extreme in reality, but I do believe that they think everything impacts them personally, in one way or another. To a Millennial, almost any event that happens locally can have a global impact. They have seen it with a viral media idea instantly canvassing the globe. The boomers have witnessed global events, but have seen that that those have little or no effect on their daily lives.

RS: Let's talk about hiring and keeping younger workers.

CM: First of all, those doing the recruiting today are always looking at the job from the recruiter's perspective. They'll say, "Here is our company. Here's our profile. We offer stability. We offer 401(k) plans. Here's why you should work here. Here is what we can offer you." That message is typically delivered from a boomer point of view. While that is appropriate to a boomer, it probably doesn't resonate with the typical Millennial. Recruiters are ignoring the point of view of the person they are trying to recruit.

RS: From your experience, which organizations are getting it right?

CM: Watch the army commercials. The U.S. Army spends an enormous amount of money learning how to talk to Millennials. They spent something like $250 million last year. They talk about what these young people will become. They talk about where the army is going to take them. They talk about the change you will see in yourself. The army also has done something pretty radical. They are getting the parents involved in their recruiting. They are telling the parents, "Parents, you've got to let go and trust us to do some more teaching." The child sees it, and the parents see it. The army has learned that parents have become "partners in life" with their children. Children and parents make career decisions together. They make purchases together. They buy homes together. In fact, the children are very influential in their parents' home purchases.

Another great organization I like is Enterprise Rent-A-Car. It is common for Enterprise to call a prospective candidate and tell that person that they would like to make a job offer, and then suggest a conference call with the candidate's parents. Enterprise wants an opportunity to discuss where their child will fit into the organization and what will happen when their child comes on board, and also to answer any questions parents might have.

RS: Fascinating. So, let's talk about how to retain this younger workforce.

CM: The key is creating a job process that comes in bite-sized career hunks. Millennials like to know what's going to happen next. Enterprise likes to talk about, "Here's what's going to happen to you when you come to work with us." They focus on the very short term. For example, they might say, "In the first three to four months, here are the changes you will see. Three months after that, you'll see the following changes. And three months after that, you will be transformed into this." There are no five- or ten-year plans. They want to get real short-term about how these people are going to change.

RS: How is performance measured? How are promotions handled?

CM: In the Enterprise case, the promotional opportunities are such that when an individual proves competency doing a task, they promote him or her on the spot. It doesn't go to a committee. There is not a minimum amount of time required. No seniority stipulations.

They believe, "If you can do it, we are going to promote you." For the first three years, there are a lot of small promotions. They have it set up so that the manager identifies the behavior they are seeking, and once the employee proves fluency in the behavior, the promotion happens immediately. The promotion is a change in title and a small change in compensation. The integrity of that process is that the company is saying, "We've seen that you can do it. We are acknowledging you can do it. Let's reward you. Let's celebrate. And now let's set the goal for your next promotion."

RS: Does this shorter term "success-and-promotion" process seem to enhance loyalty?

CM: I've noticed, in many organizations, that Millennials are not loyal to organizations or corporations. They are not loyal to the profession, or even to the career path. But they are very loyal to people. They find people they like and respect, and they stay loyal to them.

RS: What traits are they looking for in those people? In those managers?

CM: Millennials want to be with people who are advocates for them. They want to be around people who ask, "What can I do for you?" "What do you need?" "Where do you want to go?" "Who do you want to meet?" "How can I help you?" I see a trend where the advocate attitude is replacing the mentor role. The companies that adopt an attitude of *advocate*, rather than mentor, are really jumping ahead of their competition.

RS: Can you clarify what you see as the difference between a mentor and an advocate?

CM: The typical mentor says, "Let me tell you what I've done." "Let me tell you how I did it." "You are going to pick up the gems of knowledge I am about to bestow upon you." Whereas the advocate says, "How I've done it is irrelevant. What do you need, and how can we help you perform better?" The perspective shifts from *all about me* to *all about you*.

RS: Does a company attitude of *it's all about us* instead of *it's all* *about you* account for their frequent job-hopping?

CM: Yes, I believe so. Frequent and focused attention by people who really care about the employee's success is important to retention. The greatest rewards—for both parties—come from paying close attention and devoting a lot of energy to the employee's first three years of employment. If you can retain an employee for three years, the turnover rates drop dramatically. As I tell my audiences, "For three years, they live the lie. After three years, managers can relax and tell them what it's really like to live here."

The Customer Is Number Two?

Uh oh, that statement goes against everything we've ever been taught about "customer care and retention." But one company is changing the conversation about customers—and, in turn, changing the landscape with regard to attracting the best employees.

When it comes to the "employer of choice," Wegmans Food Markets, a seventy-one-store grocery chain, is ranked number one in the United States, according to *Forbes*. How did that happen? Wegmans, based in Rochester, New York, has a rather contrarian view of their customers. They preach, "The Customer Is Number Two." They understand that their employees are number one. They are the head cheerleaders of the company brand. Wegmans contends that it's the coworker's commitment and enthusiasm that brings paying customers back. Wegmans says you can post "smile at the customer" signs from Florida to Alaska, but the customer experience will not be genuine if your employees' attitudinal foundation is not sound.

What exactly does Wegmans do for their employees? They value their opinions about what products and services customers want. They encourage them to participate in the selection of the company uniform. They celebrate the smallest of achievements and customer feedback. They offer flex hours to students and working parents. They hire people who love other people and people who love to talk about good food. They smile at each other and encourage a fun atmosphere. In fact, they have so much fun at work that their attitudes can't help but transmit warm feelings to their customers.

Wegmans's customers are loyal to fun, caring people. Fresh produce is an attraction, but it doesn't have a personality.

Not Yes ... But Hell, Yes!

Fiserv is a software solutions provider to banks and other financial institutions, such as mortgage lenders and title companies. While the software products are not as sexy as something Apple might concoct, Fiserv associates flash broad smiles when they talk about the company. It's a large company with a small family feel. Lots of laughing. Lots of consoling about personal drama. Everyone I talked to had empathy and understanding for one another. They loved the idea of growing big while staying small.

At a recent convention, I stood on the floor of the trade show and overheard a couple of Fiserv employees brag about how long they had been with the company. "Forty-one years," said one. "Twenty-eight years," said another. I struck up a conversation with Doug Wilson, a sixty-two-year-old retiree of another software company and long-time admirer of Fiserv. One day he got a phone call from a buddy. Doug relayed, "I had retired comfortably, and was fishing one day a week and golfing one day a week. An old friend of mine called me up and asked me if I was bored yet. I said, 'Yeah, pretty much.' Then he asked me if I would like to come out of retirement to work with him at Fiserv. I said, 'Not yes...but hell, yes!' I've been here at Fiserv for five years, and I can't see a reason to quit having this much fun."

Want to Be Inspired?

It isn't always about the paycheck. These organizations know what matters to their teams:

- HDR Design-Build, Inc., of Omaha, Nebraska, is an engineering firm that calls upon all employees to assist the firm in quality control, project reviews, and mentoring other staff members.
- Enterprise Fleet Service is a rental car company that rewards employees for developing company and community leaders at all levels.
- Grand View Hospital in Sellersville, Pennsylvania, provides a sick-child care center on site, and offers "Grandparent Time" with children.
- Bon Secours Richmond Health Systems in Richmond, Virginia, provides childcare, summer camp, teen volunteer programs, and mobile health stations to their team members.
- KPMG is one of the nation's largest accounting firms. Based in New York, the company pays employees twelve hours annually for volunteer work in their local communities.
- Baxter Credit Union in Vernon Hills, Illinois, sponsors a Weight Watchers program; offers a fitness room, free dry cleaning, and a lactation room for new mothers; and has frequent bring-your-kids-to-work days.
- Ceridian of Minneapolis, Minnesota, an information-services company, holds regular "Ceridian Idol" contests so that the team will have more fun at work.
- Sage Products of Cary, Illinois, a health-care company, has 435 employees. They get their minds off business and the daily grind by holding salsa cook-offs, costume parties, mini-golf outings, and on-site picnics so that

employees can mingle and get to know one another in nontraditional settings.

- Analytical Graphics of Lanham, Maryland, believes strongly in a work-life balance. They provide three free meals a day, an on-site fitness center, washers and dryers, and a complimentary holiday gift-wrapping service.

There's Something Motivating about ... Honesty

Each year, I listen to about eighty senior executives' speeches.

Most aren't very good communicators. Yet, these men and women occupy chairs in the C-Suite, and are charged with giving state-of-the-union addresses at all-hands meetings. Some are low energy. Some are reading the speech for the first time. Others use too many sports analogies. Most are uncomfortable with speaking in front of people, especially when they have the task of spinning bad news into something motivational for the troops.

I met one remarkable exception.

Steve Sorensen is the president and CEO of SelectRemedy Staffing. Two years ago, Select was a small company that grew to a $500 million company through forty-plus carefully orchestrated acquisitions. When Select Staffing acquired Remedy Staffing, it doubled their gross revenue to $1 billion. They are now operating 250+ offices in thirty-five states. They are a big player, and they want to continue growing.

How do you handle the company when you double in size overnight? According to Sorensen, "The key is staying with the fundamentals that worked when we were small. So even though we are large, we want to bring a small, interactive culture to our organization. As you can guess, because we are all in a war for the best talent, the staffing industry in particular can be a difficult business."

Of course, being difficult never occurs to Steve Sorensen. He has great faith that his team will be successful. That attitude motivates every member of the workforce. But, what I found so extraordinary about Steve Sorensen is his complete candor and honesty about ... himself.

I'll give you an example.

Normally it would be taboo, bad form, and potentially alienating to refer to Bible scripture in a business setting. But being politically incorrect doesn't occur to Steve, either.

He doesn't fear the truth. He speaks directly from his heart. And, because his heart and his life are so involved with Jesus Christ and the Mormon religion, he uses biblical stories to underscore his business points. He's a very effective speaker and leader because he's authentic. He doesn't hide behind spinning rhetoric, and he doesn't sugarcoat the truth. Even though his company faced some new challenges with franchisees and the new merger, he addressed those challenges head-on and sought guidance from team members and from God. When I saw him address his twelve hundred sales representatives at their all-company meeting, he had the undivided attention of every one of them. He didn't sound like a lecturer or a fire-and-brimstone preacher. He was just a regular guy who was passionate about his mission.

I left thinking, "SelectRemedy is successful because you always know where you stand with the boss—and the boss knows where he stands with his people. Naturally, the boss expects performance, but there are no hidden agendas and no talking out of both sides of his mouth. He is predictable in the best possible way—with his ethics, his integrity, and his heart."

So Then Steve Sorensen Throws the Ultimate Curveball ...

OK, I was already impressed with Sorensen's attitude and warmth toward his team members—but what he did next blew the lid off anything I'd ever seen in a professional corporate setting.

He introduced his wife, Shannon, as his opening act!

Yup. Before he took the stage for his year-end address, he invited his wife to the stage to say a few words.

Shannon Sorensen is not a public speaker.

She doesn't even officially work in the company. But you wouldn't know it from her warm, easy style. She didn't talk about the business. And she didn't talk about her husband. She talked about one of their daughters. Apparently Shannon had come down to the breakfast table one day and was upset because her daughter hadn't cleaned her room when she was supposed to. When Shannon, rather irritated, made her feelings known, her twelve-year-old daughter said, "Mom, let's rewind. How are you today? Is there something else that is upsetting you? I'll go in and clean the room right now. Is there anything else I can do to help you?" Shannon was immediately disarmed. Her daughter's calm and empathetic response to the situation led to more love, not more anger. The parallel illuminated the business point without beating anyone over the head. "Empathy at times of stress is the best medicine for preserving and building relationships."

The story was real, vulnerable, and self-effacing. Sorensen told me at the luncheon that followed that he had had no idea what his wife was going to talk about. "I just trusted she would talk about what was in her heart."

If you want a no-cost, surefire motivator, honesty and authenticity are always relevant.

Tomorrow's Workforce Lives on a Farm?

Maybe you're looking for good people in the wrong places.

In his book, *Free Agent Nation*, Daniel Pink estimates that there are 32 million Americans who are working out of their homes, thanks to the Internet. The hiring of this vast workforce—armed with broadband connections—is being called *home sourcing*. There is a sister term, *rural sourcing*, which means the same thing, except that these folks live a little farther out of town. Exorbitant housing prices in urban areas, as well as exorbitant fuel prices, have driven many workers past the suburbs and into "the country." For this workforce, the commuting time to the cities is intolerable, so they elect to stay home and work from their computers.

This frightens most companies.

Many baby-boomer managers believe that if employees aren't sitting in their cubicles under the watchful eye of management, they will piddle around the house playing games or watching TV. But there is research to show that the opposite is true. Not only are the staff costs much lower, but productivity is actually greater. People in the call-center industry have had great success with this model. The consulting firm of Booz Allen Hamilton says home-based employee turnover is 10 percent, versus 50 percent among on-site employees.

Banking employees who work from home on mortgages or other internal banking duties love their work-at-home jobs. They enjoy the flexibility, and research supports that they actually work harder. They often put in more hours because they can work during a baby's nap or during a ball game. And they are motivated to prove that they can produce good work from home so they don't blow an ideal work situation.

Think of it selfishly. By letting smart, self-reliant people work from home, you have a greater chance of retaining a valuable member of an ever-shrinking talent force.

Retention Can't Be That Simple, Can It?

Executives tend to overthink everything. Don't overcomplicate employee retention. Human beings have ridiculously simple work needs.

Talented people don't quit wonderful jobs. Talented people quit bad bosses. Once they find a happy and emotionally rewarding work situation with a nurturing manager, they won't risk losing it. And as you will hear me say often, happy people are your most aggressive recruiting champions. They make other people jealous enough to come and work for you.

Which Companies "Get It"?

I want you to meet Dornett Wright.

She is the HR manager for DaimlerChrysler Services Truck Finance. Of all the companies I've had the privilege to see from the inside, this group is doing something truly groundbreaking regarding talent retention. Compensation is tied to several relevant factors:

- Performance numbers and goals
- Behaviors supporting the culture and mission statement
- Customer responses to their efforts
- Bright new ideas suggested
- Personal career development

The company gets everything it wants in reaching goals and encouraging cultural behavior. And the employee gets customer feedback and the opportunity to submit bright ideas. But the fresh element is the prospect for personal career development.

This is revolutionary stuff!

I'd wager this is the solution you've been looking for to improve the focus and productivity of your younger workforce. A program that helps workers discover their strengths and talents will hold their attention and nurture their desire to find fulfilling work. This program doesn't refer to just college extension courses. A lot of companies do that. No, DaimlerChrysler Services has a program called "Career Partnership" that helps to empower people to find the right job for them. Through techniques ranging from personality testing and goal-setting classes to working with a career coach and learning how to "chart your own course," this company encourages each person "to find their strengths."

Wright told me, "A lot of young people don't know what they want to do yet. Career Partnership allows them to identify their passions, skill sets, and developmental steps. We provide access to global career opportunities within the family of DaimlerChrysler companies, and we want our employees to know we value their contributions."

Richard A. Howard, DaimlerChrysler Services Truck Finance vice president, describes their philosophy of (and responsibility for) maintaining happy, productive employees—and the ensuing customer result: "Customer focus is one of our core values and defines who we are as a company worldwide. Customer focus means to take care of the needs of our internal customers—our employees—and our external customers who purchase our products and services. Take care of your customers, and they will take care of you."

DaimlerChrysler is a company that recognizes that a strong corporate foundation—and sustained profit—springs from the value of putting the right people in the right jobs. So it's no wonder that DaimlerChrysler is blowing the proverbial car doors off Ford and General Motors.

Relevant Review

You all want to hire and keep the best people. If your turnover is too high, the sprint towards your exit is telling you that you are not relevant.

How do you become more relevant in an ever-more-complex workplace?

Even though the workplace has become more complex, retaining the best people isn't as complicated as we've been led to believe.

The younger generations may seem like an enigma to you baby boomer managers, but they aren't as different from you as you think. Regardless of age and experience, great people all want the same things on the job. They want someone at work to care about them as a human being. They want opportunities to be productive in their communities. They want clear direction from the people in charge. They want to know the boundaries of integrity (even if they slightly disagree), because they want to know "the rules of the game." They want definitive instruction on their duties, opportunities to learn new things and to be proficient, and to have their performance measured often—daily, if possible—so they know where they stand. They want to work for competent, inspiring people who simultaneously challenge them and nurture them. They appreciate companies who embrace and honor a work-life balance. They like companies that provide perks such as free soft drinks, washers and dryers, and day-care options. They would like to swap jobs from time to time to see if their talents are better suited elsewhere. They would love to have the opportunity to do some of their work from home.

And—this next requirement is gigantic—they want to have fun at work.

If you don't know how to have fun at work, hire someone to show you. Feeling good on the job is critical to retention. Remember, their friends are telling them how much fun *they* are having at work, and your people want that, too.

That being said, it is important that employees get to work with people they like and respect. That's why so many relevant organizations now conduct two different hiring interviews; one interview is to determine skill level, while the second one is designed to assess a "culture fit." Organizations want to make sure a new hire will like working with you, and vice versa. These days, every hour of an employee's life is an investment of valuable time. They don't want to squander that time being miserable.

Chapter 4

There Are No One-Size-Fits-All Incentive Programs

But First, You Need to Provide the Hidden Incentive

I'll contradict myself for a moment.

There is *one* incentive that *does* seem to fit all.

The one incentive you must offer above all else, says *Entrepreneur* magazine's senior vice president and editorial director, Rieva Lesonsky. Lesonsky says most organizations overlook the most important element needed to attract and retain good people.

"Believe it or not, it's all about health-care benefits!" says Lesonsky.

Surprisingly, star talent puts health-care benefits at the top of their list of perks. They often make a gut-wrenching employment decision based on how well their family will be taken care of medically. These top performers also make the "am-I-going-to-stay-with-this-company?" decision predicated on health-care benefits. Health-care benefits speak to your employees, emotionally. Sufficient health care loudly telegraphs caring and demonstrates that a company truly cares about taking care of employees and their families.

Note: You will retain good people if they feel appreciated. Feeling appreciated and valued by an organization creates an emotional bond. Emotional bonds allow loyalty to evolve. If your people trust you to take care of them physically and emotionally, they won't leave you. It is important to remember the incredible benefit of your best people becoming your best recruiters. They will know other good people who'd like to work for you.

Reward the Hand-Off

I have been to countless meetings where someone from the C-Suite has spent hundreds of thousands of dollars on a call-to-arms conference whose goal was to encourage the divisions to network among various business units so they could extend the brand and maximize the advantages of their strengths. It is a reminder that customers see you as one brand—regardless of how many diverse divisions you have. Most business units leave these meetings with promises they will never keep.

Like it or not, unless you incentivize the process of handing business from one unit to another within the company, you can't expect results.

Why? Because most organizations are already lean, mean, and overworked. That means that at some point, every employee has an "I'm-too-busy-to-throw-off-leads/what's-in-it-for-me?" attitude.

So, Maybe You Should Copy this Company?

FC Stone is a commodities risk-management company that also of-fers service and consulting solutions. Their program, called "Lead Quest," does a brilliant job, at their annual awards banquet, of re-warding and recognizing team members who have repeatedly hand-ed the baton to another business unit. In the first place, it's the right thing to do. Secondly, it's the human thing to do. I would credit their affinity to humanity to the fact that they started out as a grain co-op. The core of this company began life working face-to-face with farmers. That core belief has remained through their growth into a publicly traded, very successful multinational company. It's not surprising that they still remember their initial success came from a "you-scratch-my-back-and-I'll-scratch-yours" mind-set.

Start scratching each others' backs and offer an incentive to do so. Then watch your organization start to actually synergize.

Do Millennials Respond to Incentives?

Great question.

We already know this work group appreciates instant gratifica-tion. And they *do* like money. But it's not always about the money for them. They would love spot bonuses awarded in time off rather than cash. Also, don't assume they want more responsibility for a job well done. They may not see *management* as a better job.

Millennials like quick goal achievement, recognition, praise, training, education, promotion, and new goal-setting. Provide opportunities for Mils to form relationships with the most talent-ed people in your workforce. They will prove to be more loyal to them. In fact, personal loyalty ranks above their loyalty to a pro-fession, corporation, or career path. To a Mil, the term *advocate* replaces the old *mentor* role for them. They want champions, not teachers. They respect competence over age. Don't constantly bore them with, "This is how we've always done things around here." They are motivated by thinking that there are better practices waiting to be discovered.

The Incentive Paradox Proves
There Are No Right Answers: Just Action

You are about to get an insider's peek at two diametrically opposed incentive studies. The first is a hospital that has too many potential employees from which to choose, yet offers a zero-bonus plan.

The second is a large title company who generates extraordinary results by offering extraordinary "prizes." What's even more interesting is that in both cases, the staff members are overwhelmingly female. So the gender comparison is apples to apples.

These organizations prove that what motivates one person does not apply to another.

What Nursing Shortage?

Hackensack University Medical Center does *not* offer any incentive programs. They also do not overpay for nurses. The salaries are comparable, but not excessive. In fact, most mobile nurses would make nearly double the dough. While they maintain a staff of about eight thousand, they need to hire roughly one thousand nurses each year; positions grow, and other nurses leave to train other hospitals. So why is it that HUMC is able to attract *twenty-eight thousand* nursing applicants for those one thousand jobs each year? A great deal of their attraction is their status as a Magnet hospital.

Magnet hospitals are hospitals that go through an exhaustive, fourteen-step evaluation by the American Nurses Credentialing

Center (ANCC) and are deemed the "cream of the crop" for recruiting and retaining nurses. It is the goal of every Magnet hospital to employ nurses who are autonomous in their control within their practice, communicate well with physicians, and have supportive leaders.

What does the Magnet board typically look for? Getting stakeholders like physicians and other nurses to "buy into" constant and open communication, mentoring, and the celebration of progress.

To attain Magnet designation, a hospital must achieve an *excellent* rating in *all* fourteen of the following standards. You can tell from this list that the Magnet board does some pretty exhaustive detective work at each hospital.

- Assessment
- Diagnosis
- Identification of Outcomes
- Planning
- Implementation
- Evaluation
- Quality of Care and Administrative Practice
- Performance Appraisal
- Education
- Collegiality
- Ethics
- Collaboration
- Research
- Resource Utilization

I talked with Joan Orseck, human resource director for HUMC. In her inimitable humility, she told me the reason she believes they attract so many talented nurses.

Joan Orseck: I like to think we are a good place to work and we take care of people. If we were doing an ad for the hospital, it would probably be, 'When *you* feel good, *we* feel good.'"

Ross Shafer: What makes Hackensack a good place to work?

JO: We give people autonomy. We pay them well. We give them opportunity for growth. We listen to people, and I think we take care of people as human beings.

RS: But do I understand correctly that you don't offer incentives and bonuses?

JO: We don't do bonuses here. We never have. And we don't use "travelers," which are nurses who are very good, but who are transient by their own decisions. We don't use nurse agencies, and we don't do any foreign recruitment.

RS: Wow. Very impressive.

JO: So right there it says a tremendous amount, and that's just been a philosophy here. We used our last agency nurse in 1989, and we haven't had one since.

RS: When you refer to travelers, this is the short-term category of employees, right? A nurse who will travel from hospital to hospital?

JO: They usually sign up for a three-month contract. They are good nurses who have just chosen to travel and see the world. Our philosophy here is that we would rather hire new grads, put the bucks into new grads, train them our way, and hope that they're going to stay with us and be good employees. We have been fortunate. Within the industry average, I think we're like in the top seventy-fifth percentile. We do surveys twice a year to make sure we stay competitive, but clearly people are coming here because of our reputation as a good place to work, a pleasant attitude, and a top-tier facility where they can learn and grow.

RS: Does that attitude come, in your opinion, from the top down, or is it at all levels?

JO: Certainly from the top down, but it exists at all levels—it really does. John Ferguson, who became our CEO in the mid '80s, has been one of the people in the "Top 100 People Making a Difference in Health Care," according to *Modern Healthcare*'s website.

RS: I heard you describe working at HUMC as an indescribable feeling.

JO: Yes, I think if you asked 95 percent of our staff, they would tell you the place has a good feeling about it. Whether you are having a good or bad day here, our staff supports each other, which is remarkable considering that we are the fourth-busiest hospital in the United States.

RS: Your occupancy rate is over 95 percent, right?

JO: It's 99.7 percent. We don't have many spare beds here.

RS: Does having twenty-eight thousand nurse applicants every year seem a bit overwhelming?

JO: Ross, in my office, right now, I probably have over one hundred applications from new grads who I will never see. And my salary recruiter has the same thing. But we are also very lucky because we can be extremely selective here, and we are.

RS: Yeah, you certainly can be. What is it that you're looking for?

JO: I always look for a good cover letter. You know, I want them to tell me in that cover letter why they want to work here, and why they think they're special. What are they going to bring to Hackensack? If I look at the application or the résumé, certainly I'm going to look at their background. If they're new grads, I want to know where they went to school, if they did an externship, etc. And if I bring them in to interview, what I want to feel from them is that they are passionate about what they do or what they're going to do, they really care, and they're going to have a commitment to us and to our patients.

RS: How long does a typical interview last?

JO: I do at least an hour with every nurse, and you can get a pretty good feel from that. You know, we have some behavioral questions, and you just watch, and you listen. And, of course, a lot of our new graduates have been externs here with us, and we take about sixty externs every summer. They're between junior and senior years. So we've got a pretty good handle on what we want.

RS: That's actually the first time I've heard "extern" as opposed to "intern."

JO: Yes. Internships are normally for the person who has graduated. They do internships as new grads for experience, or they'll do internships in a new specialty. But externships normally are those students who come between their junior and senior years. They spend the summer with us, and some of them stay on their senior year for weekends and holidays, so we get a pretty good handle on those people, you know. Do we want them here? Do they communicate well? Do they care? Are they good workers? Are they going to be wonderful nurses? You know, you watch them for a whole summer and throughout the year, and you get a pretty good idea.

RS: And because of your reputation and your standards, don't they also have a pretty clear sense that "this is my foot in the door?"

JO: Oh, absolutely. And, "I better prove myself."

RS: OK. What does the physical environment look like there?

JO: Our plant, so to speak—our hospital—is absolutely beautiful. Our lobby could be in any hotel. We just opened up a new women and children's hospital that is three hundred thousand square feet of all private rooms with windows. It is absolutely state-of-the-art and absolutely beautiful. So aesthetically, this is a wonderful place to work. But when you set that up for a patient—and I say this constantly—if you're a magnet facility, if you have this wonderful reputation, and if they walk into your hospital and it's beautiful, they have very high expectations. And you had better deliver on them.

RS: The Magnet designation is the highest honor a facility can receive. Only 165 hospitals in the United States are Magnet-certified. And you were the second one to get that award.

JO: Yes, we got it in 1995. The designation is good for four years, and we are hopefully going to be awarded our fourth consecutive designation.

RS: I have seen the list of requirements and understand the Magnet designation comes only after a long, third-party interrogation by the Magnet board. According to the board, there are fourteen "Forces of Magnetism" that attract great talent to a top-tier hospital organization. In the broadest view, what do you think the board looks for?

JO: They want to feel that your nurses are truly a part of your institution. They look at interdisciplinary relationships and the image of nursing, and they look at nurses as teachers. They also want to look at what you do in your community. The fourteen "Forces of Magnetism" are all things that they address—things like autonomy, quality improvement, quality of care, and quality of nursing leadership.

RS: I have visited literally thousands of organizations over the years, and while I've seen associations offer "certification" levels for competency, I haven't seen such an inclusive behavioral certification. How does it work? Can you describe the application process?

JO: Yes. If you want to be considered by the Magnet board, you have to fill out an extensive application in writing. And then the Magnet council comes in and does a survey of these fourteen "Forces of Magnetism," both in writing and when they come—that's what they look at. And what they really look at is, "Are you really doing what you say you're doing?"

RS: Do they "secret shop" you in a sense? Do they arrive under the cover of darkness or as a fake patient?

JO: No, we know when they're coming. And they either spend two or three days, maybe even longer now. I think they may have extended it for big institutions. But they stay a good amount of time, they meet with staff, they have lunch with the staff. They really want to talk to your worker bees ... and I mean that in the best sense, the people who are really in the trenches. You know, they want to get out there and find out, first of all, if your staff really understands what it is—what Magnet is—and are they really living it every day? The staff will tell them exactly what's going on here and how they feel about working here.

RS: But isn't that a monster evaluation when you have eight thousand employees?

JO: Yes, but even though we are that big, the answer is always the same because we have still managed to have a sense of family. The family has gotten bigger, but it's still a family, and I think that's a pretty special thing.

RS: Obviously you are dedicated to maintaining your Magnet status from hiring and behavioral standpoints. How else do you stay relevant?

JO: I think by always looking at ourselves. We take a snapshot of what we're doing, and we take a good, hard look at ourselves as we did when we first went for Magnet. We have to continue to do that. Are we giving our employees what they need? I think we certainly are, certainly in our wages, salary package, and benefits package. Those things are important, but if you'd read any surveys on nurses' salaries, we are way down the list—like fifth, sixth, seventh, eighth, whatever. It's more about their working environment, autonomy, supplies, how they're treated. They're treated as professionals.

RS: When it comes to autonomy, can you describe how a nurse would feel autonomous?

JO: Being able to feel that they can make decisions. Certainly some they can't make without a physician, but that they can make decisions, that they can feel free to talk to a physician if they disagree with an order, that they just can professionally practice their profession in a safe environment. And that they have some decision-making ability.

RS: I spoke to a group of ER nurses where they organized a lobbying effort to get an official "timeout," which they got. So now they can call a "timeout" in the ER to reorganize their instruments, clarify a wound site, or simply recheck with the surgeon for safety purposes.

JO: A good idea.

RS: Because, as you know, sometimes a doctor may be in full-steam-ahead mode, speed mode—they're talking fast or they're talking in shorthand that maybe all the nurses don't know. And it's been working really well. But that gave them such a sense of self-empowerment in the ER, and it's cutting down on errors, wrong-site surgery, and of course lowering insurance costs.

JO: I like that a lot. You should be a hospital administrator.

RS: I can't. I work very hard at avoiding hospitals.

Diamonds and Pearls and Paris, Oh My!

Now, let's flip to the polar-opposite philosophy.

I found a division of Fidelity Title that is the antithesis of the "no-bonuses" program. The Phoenix, Arizona, regional office is the top-performing office in the Fidelity family because they believe their staff members respond very well to high-value rewards.

I spoke with the always-enthusiastic Bryant Evan. Evan runs thirty-one offices with roughly 245 employees. His Maricopa County, Arizona, office is the leader and pride of the national Fidelity Title group.

Ross Shafer: Before we get into your unusual incentive program, I know you are a hands-on executive. You don't run the ship from the captain's chair.

Bryant Evan: I'm in every branch, every month, routinely, with no agenda except to go in and say, "Hi, how are you doing? How'd your son do in his Little League tournament? How is your husband doing with his broken leg? Thanks for the nice job last month. Anything you need to know from me?" And so there is no Pavlovian response to act differently. Most leaders show up and everyone thinks there's a problem, or that someone is getting fired. Everybody there, rank and file, receptionist—they all get to know me, and I get to know them. I know every one of the 244 employees on a first-name basis, as well as something personal about every one of them.

RS: So with as much face time as you get, do you also communicate through email or telephone?

BE: I don't do many emails. I prefer the telephone. I call people up and sing "Happy Birthday" to them on their birthday at the branches, and I go, "OK, you know, you've only got to go through this once a year because I have a lousy singing voice. Get ready." So it's become a company tradition and also universally dreaded. Bryant's going to sing "Happy Birthday" to you, whether you want him to or not, on your birthday. You have to understand that it's about people. It's not about product or even systems. Competition drives everybody to the point that we are talking about the same product and relative pricing. But success is about people, people, people, people. We respect people here.

RS: Let's dive into the way you reward people on merit. You start at the gold level and it goes up from there.

BE: When I came here we had twenty-five branches and we were the Tower of Babel. Nobody knew anybody or cared about anybody else. Everybody had their own branch. They had no knowledge of anybody else, what they were doing, or who they were. There was no commonality of cause. There was also no idea of excellence. Nobody knew what was expected of them, amazingly. I mean, they literally did not know what a good month or good result was. It would be like saying, "I want you to cross the goal line, but I'm not going to tell you where it is. Maybe you'll trip across it accidentally at the end of the month." So I set up monthly meetings with all my managers and my sales staff. I did an analysis of what we needed to break even and what we needed to make money. And because they generate on money, we needed $15,000 per person. We need more now because the costs have gone up, but that's how it began. I explained to them, "Hey, this is great. We can do this, and we can get what we need for the escrow managers and your people at $15,000 per person."

RS: What was the reaction to that number?

BE: Well, in some cases, I got puzzlement like, "Wow, really? That's cheap." Other people told me, "We won't ever do that." I remember one lady in particular. She ran a little four-person department, and her office was facing foreclosure. It was doing about $45,000 per month in gross revenue with four people. I said, "Let's all set goals and set a goal to aim for." I remember coming to her and saying, "Kathy, in May you did $45,000. In June you did $45,000. And in July you did $45,000. What's your goal in August?" And she said, "$45,000." I said, "Kathy, do you think your firm is average?" She said, "No, I don't think I'm average." I said, "I don't either. Why are you aiming for average? If you went out bowling tonight and your average is 150, would you walk in the door and tell your husband, 'Honey, I hope I can bowl 150 tonight'?" I said, "I'd bet you'd be saying, 'I hope I can bowl 175.'" She agreed. I said, "OK. Let's do this. Let's aim for $50,000." Kathy stood up and waved her arms and said in a very melodramatic tone, "My department will never do $50,000 in a month." And I said, "Well, OK." "It may not," I said, "but let's aim for it." And I said, "You're not going to get fired or anything. But if you don't, let's have something to aim for." Kathy, to this day, runs that same department—now a three-person department. She literally comes and apologizes to me in any month that she does less than $150,000.

RS: Explain how you came up with the various levels of achievement.

BE: First, to establish any levels of performance, we do a monthly memo. So we recap: "Here's what we did, here's how much money we made, and here's the best." And, oh, by the way, I set it up to emulate the Olympics. I said if you could do $15,000, that would be bronze; $20,000 would be silver; $25,000 would be gold. And I really thought that would be all I'd ever need. I didn't think anybody would ever get above $25,000. Here's the interesting thing: there was no bonus money on any of these levels—no consequence, other than saying, "Congratulations! One office did bronze, another office did silver, this office did gold." Nothing financial was attached.

What happened is that a few offices were already doing $15,000, so it was easy to get started with that. It was also very hard, once you start publicizing this, for another office to say, "You can't do this in Phoenix." And when they tell me that, I say, "Really? Let's call Peggy Sue up over at her branch and find out what went wrong, because they're doing it. Maybe she can tell you how she's doing it."

RS: Very simple and powerful.

BE: And I'm always on a per-person basis to make it very fair. A five-person office has just as much chance as getting there as a fifteen-person office. And I quickly found out how powerful it was, because someone called and said, "Gee, thanks acknowledging me for silver, but I didn't have six people this month. Remember 'So-and-so' is out on maternity leave? So I only had five. And if you divide by five, I actually did gold." I said, "You're right. I'm so sorry. I'll send out a correction memo that you did gold." The amazing thing was, monetarily it made no difference whether they did silver or gold. They didn't get anything for it other than kudos; it was so motivating, though, that they wanted their peer recognition, the credit, the acknowledgment of, "we really did good."

RS: But you soon outgrew the bronze, right?

BE: Yeah. We've raised the bar so much now that I've eliminated the bronze, because eventually the costs of operating went up to where we don't make money at $15,000. We now make it at $20,000. The bottom level is silver now. And virtually everybody in the company does at least silver, which will only get you an "attaboy," nothing more. And it goes to gold at $25,000. What I did when I started—I started having some offices hit silver, then hit gold. What I've always promised them was this: when the top office hits gold, I'm going to set another level. Not that I expect you to do it. Not that I'm pushing you to do it. But there always should be a mountain to climb. I frequently quote Alexander the Great as weeping when he felt he had no more worlds to conquer. So I said. "You're already exceeding my expectations ... but when we hit a new frontier mark,

I'm going to set up another level." So then when they hit gold, I set up platinum at $30,000.

RS: And by now you're making good money at these levels.

BE: Yes! I said, "You know what, we're beginning to make a lot of money. Here's what I'm going to do. Besides the 'way to go,' I'm going to give every full-time employee in that office a $250 gift card, in addition to bonuses that are also a possibility. And I'm going to give the managers a $500 gift card." Boom, we started hitting platinum. So when they hit platinum, I needed another level. So this time, I went from $30,000 to $40,000. And I said, "We'll do diamonds. And what we'll actually do is go out and buy you a diamond necklace." Most of my employees are women. We'll get them a .38 carat diamond necklace, and we'll get the managers .48, half-a-carat diamond. Boom, after a while, I'm making now $20,000 per person. When I hit $40,000 per, I've got some money to move with. Eventually somebody hit $40,000 and I thought, "I'll be damned. I never thought that would happen." I said, "OK, again, I am not expecting anyone to go higher, but I'm going to set another level: $50,000. We'll do double diamonds, and we'll double the amount of money we put in the diamond to make it nicer. And for the manager, we'll give you a one-carat, $8,000 diamond." If we make $30,000 per person in a seven-person office, I just made $210,000. So we create that level and, boom, eventually, somebody hits the double diamond. Now, I'm dazzled. I'm thinking, "Damn, I didn't think this could be done." So I said, "OK. We're not done, though, folks. Here's what we do: $60,000 is the Paris level. I'll send you to Paris round-trip, and you also take $1,000 spending money." I tell the employees they can do it any way they want. But the reward is going to be, "I get you to Paris with $1,000 in spending money." Boom, eventually, honest to God, somebody hit the Paris level.

RS: But, doing rough calculations here, you're doing really well at this point?

BE: Oh, at $40,000 per person in a ten-person office, I make $400,000. Yeah, I'm thrilled to be able to send them to Paris with that kind of profit. When they got to that level, I said, "OK, I've got to raise the bar again to the international level—say, $70,000 per person. If you hit that, we will send you anywhere in the world for two, and bring you back, and add a little more spending money." And we had fewer and fewer, but we eventually had somebody hit $70,000 per person, per month. I said, "OK, have a nice time!"

RS: No doubt you are going to have to set a new level—a new mountain.

BE: Right. I think the "universe" level is the next goal, because now I'm running out of names. But we said we've got to up the money dramatically—now we're at $80,000. And the funny part is, the office that did that was the lady I told you about earlier, the melodramatic woman who told me, "We will never!" Her branch did $80,000 per person. They did $240,000 with three people. So we gave them, of course, a ton of money, and then we just established a $90,000 level, which nobody's yet done. That's the "galactic" level. But I still have people hitting Paris and so on.

RS: So what would you say to managers who are trying to invent an incentive program based on performance?

BE: I've been in sales all of my life, but this method showed even me that people can do amazing things beyond what they think they can do. But if you asked me five, six, seven years ago, "What do you think, realistically, an office can do per person?" I probably would have said, "Once in a lifetime, maybe $40,000 or $50,000." I would have been so wrong. I would have undersold them, because I let them rise to their own levels.

RS: You also believe in daily scoring so that everyone knows what their in-house "competition" is doing every day.

BE: Yes, that's why we do the daily report. If you don't know the scores, if you don't know the goal, or if you don't know how we're doing, then how can I expect you to support the efforts?

How can I expect you to understand the decisions we might make if you have no idea what we're trying to do here? What I figured out, after a couple of years, was this: all my branches are different sizes, but branches like to compare themselves to other branches. Well, it's unfair for a five-person branch to think they can do what a ten-person branch can do. So at the very end, I put "opening per employee"—opening escrow—on the first page, and revenue per employee on the second page. This leveled the playing field, so they can say, "Hey, we're doing the best of any branch in the company." And it may be another five-person branch, because they had more openings per employee, and they have more revenue per employee. So everybody creates a positive, peer competition in which everybody sees what everybody else is doing. Everybody is measured by the same criteria, regardless of the size of the branch. They can be my best branch even though they may be the smallest branch, because we do it on a per-capita basis.

RS: OK. And you are talking about opening the escrow account and closing the escrow account as the metric? I also see you have a second page for actual revenue.

BE: Yes, on the second page, it's all about revenue. It's the revenue per person. That's the other place I get my numbers for the award levels.

RS: It seems to me that in order for this to work, your managers have to be very strong. How do you find people who really are savvy, who understand all this, and are brave enough to come up with their own goals?

BE: We are always looking for strong people. Some of the organizations want to get by cheap. They want people to do transactions. I want people to perform. We have a lot of strong personalities here, and on occasion that creates pushback, because I give them a lot of latitude. So if you give them that, legally, morally, you get the job done; I don't micromanage. You can set your branch up different than someone else's. That's fine with me. I don't have a boilerplate hiring plan at all. And when we recruit, we do it with utter honesty. We go out and say, "Hey, we have higher standards than anybody in the industry. We're proud of that. We will expect more from you than anybody's ever expected, and we will do more for you than anybody's ever done if you hit those expectations. Is that a fair situation?" They say, "Yeah. What do you expect from me?" "Well, you're an es-crow officer. We expect $20,000 per person. Do you have an as-sistant?" She says, "Yeah." And I say, "OK. Well, we need at least $40,000 per person per team, and it mainly takes three to six months to get there because you have to rebuild your business. But is that within a reasonable period of time? Do you think you can do that?" Well, the winners go, "I've been doing that all my life." And I say, "Well, then, here's the other good thing: we don't do anything on seniority." People always ask about job se-curity. Oh, yeah, most companies do "last one in, first one out," which is another horrible plan. I say, "We don't do anything on seniority. Not promotions, not layoffs, nothing. In fact, if you're worried about security, let me ask you this: do you think you'll be in the upper 50 percent of my employees?" Well, every good person I've ever interviewed says right away, "Yeah, I'm always in the top 10 or 20 percent. Sure, I'll be in your top 50 percent." I say, "Great. I've never in my life had a time where I laid off 50 percent of my employees. You're good to go. You have exactly the same job security as I have." They always say, "Oh, thanks. You have, what, twenty-three years of service here?" I say, "Look, I have no contract. I have no guarantee. I'm here as long as I'm an asset. I'll have security and success with the company. My security's in my own hands. We're going to put your security in the best possible hands: yours."

Fidelity associates are gently challenged to push their own en-velopes farther than they ever thought possible. No pressure, just enthusiastic encouragement. When employees hit stretched sales targets, it's like they've hit the lottery. Bump into the gold level, and you get a pair of one-carat diamond earrings. Hit the universe level, and your entire team is whisked off to Paris, France, for a week with all expenses paid. Without question, this company is able to entice self-described ordinary people into consistently delivering extraordinary performance.

What approach will work for you? What incentives will be relevant to your team? Have you asked them?

Don't "Incentivize" the Wrong Goals

Incentives need to be linked to relevant goals. The relevant goal should be customer retention, because loyal customers cost you nothing in extra marketing. If loyal customers continue to be treated well, they become your unpaid sales force for driving new referrals. Most organizations understand this premise. For some reason, we've run into a lot of poor incentive models in the banking industry.

A common misstep in the banking industry is the practice of basing incentives on the number of mortgages a sales rep can land. Mortgages are important because the length of the loan is so long. By its nature, your customer is locked into you for ten, fifteen, or thirty years. Banks know that mortgages open the door to offering that customer the full breadth of your products. The mortgage is the key that unlocks the rest of your customer's wallet. Once you have a solid relationship based on the mortgage, you can talk to the customer about 401(k), ancillary retirement vehicles, and other financial services. Unfortunately, what banks often do is reward their reps on the basis of bringing in *new* mortgages, with little or no reward or recognition for *retaining* those customers who hold a mortgage with the bank.

Losing 70 Percent of Our Customers
Is Still a Net Gain, Right?

I have done some work for a chain of banks where they boasted that their Internet sales and marketing efforts were able to attract one thousand new customers per month. I asked a senior leader, "Of the one thousand new customers you sign, how many do you retain for six months or longer?" He beamed, "We keep about three hundred of our new customers, which is still a nice net gain, right?" When I asked him why those other seven hundred left, he said, "They said we weren't friendly enough."

Ah, there's the big clue. This bank is doing something well enough to attract the customers, but is not able to retain them. Was the not-too-friendly factor the turnoff? I told the bank president I had personally been to three branches, and none of the tellers or managers smiled at me—or at anyone, for that matter. He told me, "Yes, I know. The only people who smile are on our website. But here we are very serious about not making any mistakes. Smiling is not a priority."

Here's a lesson for all you bankers out there. You don't get extra credit for being accurate. Customers expect you to get their money right. That's mandatory. But if your website portrays friendly people, then as a customer I interpret that as a promise. I expect to meet other smiling people when I visit my local branch. If you want to keep your customers, you have to deliver on your promises, real or implied.

Bankers, are you hearing this? Since some of your brethren are probably blowing it, there are enormous opportunities for you to be innovative and relevant—and to gobble up market share.

Relevant Review

I hope you all accept that a strong health-care program is an incentive must. A catastrophic illness has such unpredictable consequences; you need to eliminate their worst fears immediately and realize that good people consider this "a perk worth changing jobs for."

Secondly, incentives only work when you can see higher performance directly related to giving them something extra. Don't incentivize metrics that don't mean anything to anyone. Some people are motivated by money. Others are motivated by recognized certification. Yet others perform better with shorter work hours or the ability to do work from home.

You'll have to do some serious investigating to discover what your people respond to. Then, stay on top of your incentive programs, and adapt them as people's interests and motivations change. During the summer of 2008, with $5.00-per-gallon gasoline, a gas gift certificate would have been a very relevant incentive.

Chapter 5

What's the Future of Training Departments?

Are Training Departments Too Expensive?

What good are training departments?

I see many companies whacking the training budget because they don't want to take people off the job to attend a class or watch a training film. But before you turn this department into a self-service library, understand that your company will die if you don't take training seriously. Ongoing training is as important to you as product and service pricing. Operational methods, cultural shifts, and generational transitions within your workforce require perpetual training and retraining.

Just keep in mind that not everybody learns the same way.

How Do People Want to Be Trained?

One of the most revolutionary outcroppings of the digital world is the variety of training methods available. We all know some people are "auditory learners" and others are "visual learners." As a leader, it is your responsibility to know which members of your team respond better to one method over another.

Secondly, if you want to remain relevant, you should offer your staff the option to be trained via videotape, DVD, live learning, online streaming video, or even the iPod. Yes, the iPod.

The iPod Becomes a Training Tool?

You can enjoy lower costs and higher training results when you adapt your training methodology to employ "tools" the younger workforce already knows how to use.

"Pals," a seventeen-unit chain of hamburger stores in the northeastern United States, enthusiastically uses the iPod for employee training. They create podcasts, and they've found that they can reduce the training cycle from three weeks to two weeks by allowing the content to be available on demand via the iPod. Dan Evans, director of in-store training, says, "The kids already own the technology—and if they don't, we buy it for them. They love learning that way."

Training Doesn't Work Because It's Irrelevant.

One manager complained to me, "By the time we train our employees, the market has changed—or we've merged with some other company that has its own ideas about training. It's a hamster wheel, and we never know if we're jumping on or bailing off."

Well, you can't stop mergers and acquisitions from changing your career direction. Those decisions are probably not within your job control. Besides, you have enough to think about. Your organization is scrambling to get your "e-commerce piece" in place, correct? Oh, and aren't you supposed to be figuring out how to import to China?

So, what good is having a formal training department if they can't keep up with so many unpredictable shifts? The simple answer is that training needs to be both specific and general. Specific training must remain flexible in method, yet specific to detailed performance of duties. General training should be designed to maintain healthy and fun attitudes within a dynamically changing culture.

In any case, ongoing training is essential to keep the profit train moving, whether you are in a merger or acquisition transition or not. Let me offer an example of how a company can derail itself by ignoring the obvious.

"Your Business Card Is Obsolete"

Many years ago, I was working for a struggling CBS-TV affiliate station. We were all going through extensive procedure training. One day, the training was interrupted because an all-hands meeting was called. The general manager walked into a room of about 150 of us and said, "I have some peculiar news for you. First, as of today, your business cards are obsolete. We've been sold."

All training was abandoned immediately. We all waited to see what would happen when the parent company's new troops were folded in. It became a dangerous recipe for irrelevance as the whole company shut down "to await instructions." The strange thing was that the newly folded-in troops didn't know what was going on, either. Productivity ground to a halt, and both the old and new organization were paralyzed without a transition plan. What was already a struggling operation became slow as sludge to react to market conditions. At the time we were the number-two station in the market. Almost overnight we slid to number three.

How Could the Sludge Factor Have Been Prevented?

First of all, understand from a management perspective that your employees are fragile people. It's human nature for them to expect the worst when their routine is disrupted. Set the tone by talking about the positive effects of the merger. The fact is, most companies are acquired because they are doing something pretty cool. That's what makes them attractive as a takeover target.

Secondly, the parent company should have taken two minutes to ask management what training was currently in place. Then they could have formed a plan to either replace the training with their model, or dovetail current training with *their* best practices. The worst thing to do is stop all training for an "investigative evaluation." Training departments that are effective never stop operational training just because the boss moved down the hall.

Training and Inspiring Part-Timers Who "Rock!"

How many part-timers can you use to boost profits and enthusiasm? Probably more than you think.

Because so many organizations strive to get (and stay) lean, sometimes they forget that the most economical solution is to hire a workforce of trainable employees who can offer valuable skills— and who don't want to become full-timers. Such is the case with the Seattle Supersonics basketball team. The Sonics, who recently relocated to Oklahoma City, became one of the most successful training and customer-centric cultures in all of professional athletics during their forty-plus years in Seattle.

I spoke with Pete Winemiller, vice president of customer relations for the Sonics. Pete's methods have now been copied throughout the NBA, and he is frequently asked to speak to other organizations who want to clone his secret formula.

Ross Shafer: To get a sense of scale here, how many people does it take to host a Sonics basketball game?

Pete Winemiller: We need 510 employees to show up for work before we can roll a basketball out and play the game. And that number wouldn't include players, coaches, and trainers. Now, of those 510 employees, only about 30 are full-time Sonics employees.

RS: The rest are part-time?

PW: Yes, 400+ people who work part-time for the Sonics, or who don't work for the Sonics at all. When you rent a building like we do, you inherit relationships with crowd-management people, concessions, and other pre-assigned work groups.

RS: People who work for the city or some private organization?

PW: Yes. The concessionaire, Aramark, for example, which is the single largest group, is probably about 300+ employees working food and beverage—fine dining, concessions, culinary, or whatever it may be. There are 125 or so ushers, most of whom work multiple games or any one of more than one hundred annual events in that building.

RS: So how do you rise to the challenge of training and motivating people who don't necessarily work under your roof every day?

PW: The first concept was to get everyone on the same page. We had to convince Aramark that we should be the ones doing the training; which we eventually did. Two years ago, Aramark said, "We're going to allow you to develop, deliver, and then reward training that our employees will be successful in implementing."

RS: Pretty trusting of them to turn that over to you.

PW: Well, we work closely together. They knew we were serious about this. And now they have seen how successful it has been. We live by the quote, "You are the single most important person in the organization for creating a positive experience for the fans."

RS: A positive experience that's *not* based on whether your team won or lost that night, correct?

PW: Yes, the best emails I get are, "We lost by 30 points, but everywhere I went, I was taken care of." As far as I know, we can't guarantee a win [*laughs*]. If we happen to lose, I can't bring the team back the following morning to play the game over again for you. But our fans can still have a great experience regardless of the final score.

RS: I know you believe the part-time employee is more significant than even ... you?

PW: Absolutely. I tell the part-time employees that I've been a Sonics member now for thirteen seasons, but if I didn't show up for a month, I really think the Sonics staff would think to themselves: "Pete's not here for four weeks. We can get by." But if I don't have frontline staff here for four weeks—or for four days, for that matter—I can't conduct business.

RS: And you also impress upon part-time employees that they could be the reason that season tickets get renewed?

PW: I do! Let's say you ask the question, "Why do people choose not to renew their season tickets?" That could be a long list of answers. But let's say you ask, "Why wouldn't someone renew his or her season tickets?" The answer gets more narrow. We can't control the win or loss of the game, but we *can* control the answers to questions like, "How was I treated?" and "How do I feel about people who I have to work with?" It may be about how you can relate to the people in your section, or another person who sits next to you. We stopped worrying about wins and losses. Instead, we sincerely asked part-timers, "What do you do?" "How can we help you?" We found that by showing genuine interest in them, we were empowering employees to be successful problem solvers.

RS: What kind of "empowerment?"

PW: We wanted to give our employees complete and absolute authority so that if anything came up, they had the ability to solve it without having to go to anybody. I'll give you an example. Say you see a guy walking down the concourse, and his sweater has a nacho cheese-sauce stain on it. Well, you've just defined a problem. How do you solve that problem? Well, you have many answers to this question. The answer may just be simply to help him get the cheese sauce off his sweater. Or maybe you realize that that was his meal for the night, and you go ahead and buy him another order of nachos. Or it might be getting him a giveaway T-shirt from behind the counter. Or actually escorting him into the shop and getting him a sweatshirt as a replacement—no questions and no cost to the fan. Any answer you pick was the right one, because you are the immediate authority. In our case, part-timers know more about what is happening at that moment than I do as the vice president—or anyone else in the organization.

RS: Some organizations might think it's too risky to allow part-timers to have that much control.

PW: I get that all the time. They'll say, "That's crazy! You are going to empower 510 part-time employees to give away the store?" I can tell you that nobody is giving away hot dogs and free popcorn to their nephews and nieces. Instead, we get great and reasonable resolutions because we embrace employees' concerns. And we show them that "we trust you, and you wouldn't be here if we didn't trust you, and we want you to use that power."

RS: Training people to do the right thing.

PW: Yes, we teach people to do whatever is in the customer's best interest. We believe that 70 percent of our guests will come back and do business with us again if we resolve a problem in their favor. But 95 percent will do business with us again if we resolve the problem in their favor *on the spot*!

RS: Tell me how you developed your training acronym, CLICK.

PW: I wanted to develop a five-step mnemonic device for maintaining an attitude. I liked CLICK because when you say that you "clicked" with someone, everyone knows you made an immediate personal connection. It's easy to understand. CLICK is an acronym for Communicate Courteously; Listen to Learn—not listen to respond; Initiate Immediately; Create Connection; and, last but not least, Know Your Stuff. Let's say I do the other four—I've been a great listener, I'm courteous, and I initiate immediately—but I can't answer a question like, "Hey, where's the closest men's restroom?" or "Where's the closest ATM machine?" Well, if I send you to the women's restroom when you wanted to go to the men's restroom, then I really don't have the ability to be successful. So that's the idea of CLICK.

RS: And this has been effective with part-time employees?

PW: Very much so. We walk around with little CLICK chips—they look like poker chips—and when we spot someone who is practicing one of the CLICK steps, we hand out a chip. If you collect four chips, you are entitled to different prizes. The CLICK chip really became two ways to solve a problem. First, it became a prop for a manager to use to bridge a conversation, to walk up to an employee who is deserving of the chip and say, "I want to give you something." It's an easier way to make that connection. Secondly, it was to say, "I noticed that you were doing something, and I want to reward it. I noticed that you were kneeling down to make eye contact with a child and you were creating connection, and I want to give you this CLICK chip for that." The idea is that the chips are not to reward exceeding expectations, but to reward people for fundamentally great guest care.

RS: And it's a way to reward people unexpectedly and spontaneously.

PW: Exactly. See, we respect our people. We accept the fact that people working part-time jobs are working to be successful, and so what is the best way to do that? It's to ask them to have quick wins—not asking them to reinvent themselves. And for us to be confident in knowing that we are going to set them up for success.

Again, the concept of the quick win was *not* to exceed expectations, but to provide fundamental guest care consistently.

RS: But you do reward people for exceeding expectations as well?

PW: Oh, yeah! You need to reward your superstars! We hire a shopping company to come as a third-party observer to give us another perspective. This third party is telling us, "This person didn't just show me where the restroom was located, they didn't just give me an open-hand point to it—they walked me to the restroom. And when I asked them a question, they engaged me in conversation." We then reward those individuals on the main basketball floor during a game at the arena—center court—and we put their face and name on the Arena Vision big screen. The PA announcer booms their name over the sound system, and we give them a pin that says, "100 percent Guest Care," in a velvet bag. We take their picture, and they get a copy of the picture. It's become a high honor.

The U.S. Navy Goes Corporate?

If you are an ensign in the Navy and your admiral says jump, you jump. No questions. No arguments. You jump as high and as often as he barks.

I've met a lot of CEOs who admire that structure.

As you probably know, the armed forces are the supreme "command and control" environment. The senior officer gives orders, and the subordinates follow them without argument. That's how decisions are made when you need to win wars. But imagine what happens during peacetime, when the military is interfacing with civilians—rebuilding cities, restocking businesses, and restoring the economic order. Take Iraq, for example. Think of how the military is working with that country to restore everything from roads to department stores. "Command and control" can't give orders to civilians. They have to give way to cooperation, empathy, cultural differences, work-ethic discrepancies, and un-tenable time pressures.

The U.S. Navy and the U.S. Air Force are acutely aware that military leaders need to learn and to adapt their behaviors and op-erational procedures. They need to mirror the ways in which cor-porate leaders and decision makers get things done.

At the forefront of that training is Jeffrey Munks. Munks is a former San Jose police officer who has launched and sold several successful public companies. He also has an extensive teaching background, and is a consultant to China's leading kindergarten through high school education portal.

I asked Jeff to describe his program for training admirals to be CEOs.

Ross Shafer: Let me just start by asking about your capacity with the U.S. Navy.

Jeff Munks: Right now, I work as a senior program manager for the navy's executive learning office. It's a relatively new organization. We started in April 2002 with the appointment of a retired three-star admiral, Phil Quast. Phil hired me at that time to serve as his deputy in an effort to create something that had never existed be-fore: a career-long professional development continuum for naval senior leaders, both admirals and their civilian counterparts in the executive service.

RS: I always think of senior military leaders as being strong, confi-dent, and able to handle any task. Why do you think it was neces-sary to form an executive learning office?

JM: It was started by Admiral Vern Clark, then chief of naval op-erations. Admiral Clark felt that across his most-senior leadership teams—specifically, his top 230-some admirals, which included great fighter pilots, great ship drivers, great mariners, great logisti-cians as lawyers and doctors—few had many skills in the art and science of business. And at that most senior level, the majority of the senior leader positions are much more analogous to what the corporate sector would probably describe as C-suite occupants: a CEO, a CFO, a COO, a CTO, a CIO, etc. He knew he still had about nineteen or twenty billets—admiral assignments—whose principle concerns were focused on war fighting. The vast majority of those assignments were focused on managing the $120 billion annual enterprise and the almost one million people—uniformed military, reserves, civilians, and contractors—who keep the navy moving on a day-to-day basis. So he chartered our small group to come up with a strategy, a plan, and a process for providing senior leaders with the kinds of learning opportunities that would enable them to develop greater business acumen.

RS: How did you start such a massive project?

JM: What we did was we tried to stay focused on the intersection of enterprise requirements and individual needs. That orientation or philosophy led us to engage with Rand Corporation on a very expensive study of every single admiral and senior civilian position in the navy. From admiral down to each of those individual incumbents, we asked, "What are the knowledge, skills, and abilities required to succeed in your job?" We documented all of those and used them to create something that we call a "job book." That job book is available online in a password-protected, secure environment that enables admirals to look at jobs that they may be headed toward, and see exactly how other senior leaders describe the skills and abilities required for success. And if they're lacking in any of those areas, they can come to our group—the executive learning office—and I will work with them to find a program that will help improve or increase their confidence in that given skill area.

RS: Did you find any instances where the job that they thought they knew how to do wasn't what they really needed to know?

JM: I guess I could sum it up best by just saying that it's recognition that "what got you here" isn't going to "get you over there." They need to be exposed to different skill sets than what they come to the table with. When they take a new job, the rules are different, the environment is different, the expectations are different—and the navy is not unique in this regard. In both the public and private sectors, in every domain, and in every type of organization, people, particularly the higher they get in leadership, often find themselves in a position where they're lacking some of the specific competencies that are required for success.

RS: Can you describe how this works? Do you get all of the admirals together from all over the world?

JM: We start with every new group of admirals and SESs who are appointed each year.

RS: Can you clarify what the SES designation means?

JM: Sure. That's "Senior Executive Service." Those are the civilian equivalents of admirals. Each year, about forty-five new SESs and about forty-five new admirals are selected, and they come to our group for a two-week, intensive, residential experience. It's called the "New Flag Officer and SES Training Symposium." During those two weeks, we give them a very intensive exposure to what the navy characterizes as its live critical enterprise competencies. Those competencies include human capital management, financial management, IT management, change management, and, finally, leadership. But leadership is contextualized against those other four competencies. That's simply an acknowledgment of the difference in leadership requirements that attend to the most senior leadership level. In other words, when a naval officer is the captain of a ship at sea, there's absolutely no question that everybody on board is going to respond fully and immediately to every command, every request, and every suggestion that comes down from that captain.

RS: The "command and control" model.

JM: Exactly. But when that same individual becomes the admiral in charge of a shore installation with five thousand people, half of whom are union-represented, and he issues the order to jump, the response in that environment may well be, "Why don't you talk to my shop steward about that?" So the context of leadership is enforced greatly by where the individual is, what their assignment is, and what their command entails. We spend a good deal of time during that two-week orientation on those core competencies. We teach enterprise competencies for new senior leaders.

RS: Do they get everything they need in this two-week immersion, or are there "next level" courses?

JM: Within the next year or two, after appointment to senior leadership, we ask them to come back for another intensive, ten-day residential program that we call the "executive business course." That course has a deeper focus on those enterprise competencies. It isn't dissimilar to the way one would build a degree from undergraduate to a graduate-level education.

RS: A "deeper dive."

JM: Yes, it's a deeper dive into the specifics of those topics. And we generally build that experience around an actual naval challenge or opportunity—something that is confronting the enterprise at that time. So we'll take advantage of those thirty-five senior leaders and put their creative talent and energy to work on trying to frame a solution, or approach, to an issue that has been teed up by the senior-most leadership in the navy. It is a topic around which to base the study on new theory, new practice, and a new approach in those core enterprise competencies.

RS: It's tricky to narrow down a list of core competencies, because some organizations can make a grocery list of eighty or one hundred things that they say they do well.

JM: You and I have both seen those kinds of numbers and higher, and it just baffles me how you could expect an individual in your organization to remember 129 competencies.

RS: I've never seen it work in practice—only on paper.

JM: So what we've tried to do is to "steal" all of the competencies one might be able to articulate down to the lowest and broadest common denominator, and we come up with the five that I shared with you.

RS: Do one or two become "class favorites?"

JM: Not really. Over time, there seems to be an almost equal interest expressed in all of them, and I think that that is a testament to the value that the individual leaders attribute to each of those critical competencies. I mean, this is an enterprise that runs on technology, so how can you downplay the importance of information technologies, information security, information assurance, and the managing of that entire arena?

RS: And the scope of their responsibilities rivals some of the world's largest corporations.

JM: Yes. To put it in perspective, the U.S. Navy is an enterprise that consumes now about $125 billion in taxpayer money every year. So there's a tremendous interest in learning to be better stewards of the public funds, and in the entire realm of governments and fiduciary issues. If you're not an MBA, if you're not an accountant, how do you learn to speak financial language sufficiently well to be able to engage your comptroller and dissect a spreadsheet? How can you build and manage a budget, and understand the essential color of money? How do you distinguish between the different types of dollars that are appropriated or provided or come into play in dealing both internally and with vendors, and contractors, and suppliers? And the same goes for human capital management. It is a very, very competitive marketplace for human talent out there. And the navy wants very much to be able to retain its best and brightest. They want to attract the best and brightest, both in its enlisted and its officer ranks. The difficulty is compounded by a mobile workforce that has more options in terms of having the ability to change jobs, to work from wherever you want over the network, and to literally be the master of your own destiny. How does the navy not only stay competitive, but become the persistent employer of choice for the best and brightest talent that's out there?

RS: OK, so how do you accomplish all of that?

JM: By making everyone aware and skilled in the art and honor of human capital. The whole issue of attracting and retaining top talent is one of the central themes in conversations that we have in our classrooms. And I don't think it's so much about the *solutions* as it is about *approaches*: the way you look at your commitment to treating people fairly, appropriately; giving them an opportunity to grow and learn with their jobs and with the organization; keeping meaningful challenges in front of them so that they don't get stale or perceive that their environment is getting stale. These days, talented people stay with relevant organizations that treat them well. The navy is no different than Microsoft or Intel. We all are trying to get the same people.

Relevant Review

Training is mandatory. Don't even consider cutting back on your training department. Your people deserve to know what you expect from them. If you are doing your job correctly—by innovating your operations and keeping your finger on your employees' collective pulse—you will find yourself in a constant state of training and retraining. Training and refining is the only way you will be able to maximize your changing best practices.

Review your training modules today.

Which of your procedures are no longer viable? What are you keeping in your library that is outdated? What classes or books need to be rewritten? What are you doing on videotape or DVD that might be better adapted to an iPod or a Livescribe pen? Are there online solutions for what you do? Can you set up desktop videoconferencing for some kinds of training meetings?

To be relevant, understand that the medium can sometimes improve the message.

Chapter 6

Stop Spending Money on Marketing and Promotion

Stop Spending Money?

Advertising doesn't work the same way anymore.

The so-called "new media" has scared the pixels out of television and radio stations. Traditional general-interest newspapers are scrambling to stay alive. The eyes and ears have migrated to follow revolutions like TiVo and other DVRs, YouTube, MySpace, Facebook, Wikipedia, and our own site, YourBizTube.com, in which any business can add relevant best practices pertaining to hiring, retention, marketing, and customer relations. We want a resource to help business owners, managers, and employees become more innovative by cross-pollinating ideas from other organizations.

If you are paying long, green cash for TV advertising, you want people to see the ads. With TiVo, your prospective customers can elect to bypass your commercials with the click of their remote. While TiVo won't say exactly how many units they've sold, it is estimated that there are only about 750,000 TiVo Series 2 and Series 3 units in use today. TV viewing is going through a violent metamorphosis. You can buy your favorite TV episodes and play them on your video iPod during your morning commute. Cable channels offer "on-demand" viewing, so if you miss a program, you can catch it whenever you have time. It's pretty nice to be able to sit down and watch an entire season on a rainy day—without commercials.

YouTube is even more spectacular. YouTube accounts for nearly 30 percent of all media viewing in the United States. College students are even more engaged, investing 50 percent of their media viewing time in YouTube.

What's interesting about YouTube is that it isn't just about funny video clips you can email to your friends. YouTube has become a video repository for information and instructional videos. If you want to know how to install a sink, play the piano, or cut your own hair, you can find a YouTube video—or possibly a thousand of them—on the subject! For example, it's almost impossible to believe that there are eight thousand videos posted about the Federal Reserve System. One nine-minute video had thirty thousand views! If you do a search for your favorite presidential candidate, you can see that their messages reach hundreds of thousands of viewers. The presidential parodies, such as "Obama Girl"—a spoof music video of a girl who allegedly has a crush on Barack Obama—scored even higher. This homemade video had been viewed nearly 9 million times on YouTube in the first twelve months since its posting in June 2007!

You need to start thinking about how you can use YouTube and other video-sharing media as a promotional marketing tool. There is also a new site devoted to the business-only audience. YourBizTube.com specializes in collecting videos on motivation, hiring, training, marketing, and cool innovations. It also offers the ability for you to upload your own best or fresh practices.

Learn e-Marketing from Bob Dylan

Bob Dylan is a stellar example of how you can use new media to widen your market share.

In August 2006, Bob Dylan released an album titled *Modern Times*. His goal was to reach a younger audience (or at least younger than Bob, who was sixty-five at the time). Dylan brilliantly positioned his album's marketing at the epicenter of relevance. He built an enormous MySpace page replete with fan forums, pictures, music downloads, and more. He aligned partnerships for distribution in Starbucks and Victoria's Secret stores. He did a commercial for Apple's iTunes and accepted a weekly radio gig on XM Satellite radio. Dylan became the oldest living person ever to have an album enter the *Billboard* charts at No. 1, selling 192,000 copies in its first week of release in the United States. The album also reached No. 1 in Canada, Australia, New Zealand, Ireland, Denmark, Norway, and Switzerland. It debuted at No. 2 in Germany, Austria, and Sweden, and reached No. 3 in the United Kingdom and the Netherlands. *Modern Times* has been enormously successful because Bob Dylan is still brilliant and has cleverly immersed himself in myriad digital outposts.

But What If You Aren't Bob Dylan?

You don't have to be a rock star. Organizations such as Jiffy Lube, Intel, Apple, the Phoenix Suns, and others are taking advantage of this free (for now) digital marketing universe. Because each video has a counter, companies can instantly judge if their "posts" are relevant. Cool videos can get circulated via email in seconds, like a virus—hence the phrase, "the video went viral." People click or don't click, depending on the level of cool.

Here's another tip about YouTube viewership: if you post a video, don't make it too slick. The homemade look is more effective in this medium. It looks more spontaneous and original. The upside for you is that you can actually do product and service testing in front of 100 million people before you invest any real dollars.

So What Are You Waiting For?

This is all free, by the way.

So you have no excuse to procrastinate about posting your videos on www.YouTube.com or www.YourBizTube.com.

Create a MySpace page or build a Facebook page.

Write a complete, informative story on Wikipedia about you and your organization. In fact, put this book down and do it right now before you forget.

I'll wait for you to come back.

Relevant Marketing Is Very Personal.

Your customers want nano-marketing—directed specifically *to them*

When cable TV provided enough channels to create niche-market TV, broadcasting became known as narrowcasting. When the Internet made user-generated content available to anyone with a computer, nano-casting programs were created that appeal to a handful of specific viewers.

One-on-one customization is the most personal and most powerful form of marketing. Enhance your customers' personal identity. Fuel their personal "brand," and you are immediately relevant to them.

More than ever, what your customers and clients wear, drive, eat, and drink identifies who they are. Personal branding blares, "This is who I am. Get to know me." One young worker I met said, "If you want to really know who I am, check out my cell phone ringtone."

Do You Have a "Jones" for Yourself?

Ever gotten a printed T-shirt with your name on it?

Almost every shopping mall features a retail store that will engrave your name on a mug or scan your picture onto a T-shirt. That's personal. But Jones Soda in Seattle, Washington, takes personalization to a whole different level. Jones Soda gives you the opportunity to get your picture on their soda cans and distributed throughout the world. Yes, you can submit a photo to Jones Soda online, and they will consider pasting it on their products for global distribution. How cool is that?! Do you think you would tell your friends? Of course you would. Or, if you don't want to wait for the "Jones committee" to judge your genius, you can upload your favorite picture to www.MyJones.com and order a twelve-pack of *you* for your next party. What's more fun and relevant than a soda can featuring your own picture?

I think we all agree that it's brilliant, but how did the Jones people think of it? It wasn't intentional. They did it for survival.

When Jones Soda first started out, they couldn't get the mainstream distribution that the leading soda companies already had locked up. So they focused on tattoo shops, body piercing parlors, and skate shops. Word spread until they built a grassroots following by being exceptionally relevant to their customers.

This kind of reverse thinking is disrupting how we look at marketing. No longer does a marketer have to stir the hearts of their audience through an admired celebrity spokesperson. Remember the "Be Like Mike" ad campaign? It was a Nike slogan that sent armies of teenagers to the nearest athletic shoe store in the '80s to buy the latest edition of the "Air Jordan" sneakers. Today, it's more likely your customers would prefer to see a private campaign that shouted, "Be Like Me!"

Does This Mean the Death of Celebrity Spokespeople?

Probably.

The "celebrity" of tomorrow … is *you*.

The brand that resonates most with people today is their own *personal brand*. An argument could be made that regular people are elevating *themselves* to celebrity status. We can all create a personal identity by downloading unique cell phone ring tones. We can buy cars online that can be totally customized. Ferrari lets you not only select the interior and exterior colors, wheels, tires, transmission, and gauge colors, but the exact color of seat stitching. NIKE ID allows you to design your own, one-of-a-kind, personalized NIKE ID head-to-toe outfit (see story below). Apple's iPod organizes your music per *your* request in easily accessible playlists that *you* design and label. Of course, MySpace is the ultimate personal identity storefront that enables you to display every square inch of your world with personal photos, videos, and MP3s. MySpace also is an opportunity for you to create your own "customer base" by enticing hundreds or thousands of "friends" into your world. Comedian Dane Cook's concert and movie career exploded in popularity when his "friends list" topped 900,000. With a quick click of the mouse, he could tell his legions of fans where he would be performing and sell out the nation's largest concert halls.

What's more, in the MySpace world, the highest honor for your friends is to enshrine them on your front page among your "Top Friends." Your best friends will be ecstatic that you've publicly recognized *their* sense of personal identity by giving them preferential status.

What are you doing to make your customers and clients feel personally valued?

Nike Shifted the Paradigm
Before Someone Else Shifted It for Them

It is worthwhile to "go deep" with Nike because what they have done has been quite revolutionary in retail personalization.

Nike still hires celebrity athletes to promote their brand, but they also acknowledge the self-branding phenomenon. While some people want to brand themselves with a personalized cell phone ring tone or customized soda drink, Nike allows you to design your own athletic shoes. I mean design the colors, design the fabric, and even design the name tag.

If you steer yourself to their NIKE ID website, you will be able to choose from a wide selection of fully customizable athletic shoes, apparel, and accessories. After selecting the item you like best, you can fully customize the colors and design of the product. As you walk through the online design process, the product comes to life in your favorite colors and fabrics. Change it as often as you like. Once you are satisfied with your customized design, you can add the ultimate personalized touch by inscribing your name, your school nickname, a personal mantra or credo, or virtually any words you want the world to see.

Due to its great success, the site has grown to include roughly a hundred customizable products. This is a tribute to the idea that people know what they want and love, which is to buy from and be loyal to companies that value their individual desires.

Relevant Review

Spending marketing money on your old tried-and-true ways probably isn't giving your company the return it used to. In fact, your customers and clients may have "vacated the premises" in some cases. Explore all of your new media options and look for new customers, clients, and patients in areas you hadn't considered before. There are so many free opportunities for spreading your message: YouTube, MySpace, Facebook, Wikipedia. Why not take advantage while you can?

I'm frequently asked if YouTube or MySpace actually converts views into dollars.

Maybe this next example will convince you.

I met a caricature artist named Dan Dunn whose daughter posted a four-minute video of her dad painting a portrait of Ray Charles—except you didn't know it was Ray Charles until he rotated the canvas 180 degrees. The surprise is delightful. In one year, more than 12 million people have seen that video clip, and now Dan is in wild demand as a headliner for corporate functions. He told me he paid off his house and bought his wife a new Lexus. And his fees keep climbing because YouTube is working for him 24/7.

This begs the question, "How long will YouTube be free?" Can you imagine the revenue model they would have if two hundred thousand million people a day had to pay $1 to view or upload videos? Never happen? Nobody thought pay-TV would take off, either.

Your customers and clients want you to provide them with a more personal experience. If you can adapt your products and services to offer individualization, the return is highly emotional. Loyalty only follows the emotional connection you have made with your customers and audience.

What product or service do you do sell that could be so personal that it enhances a customer's *personal* brand sense?

Chapter 7

Customer Service Is Obsolete

"We Want to Be the Nordstrom of Pest Control!"

I can't tell you how many times my clients have said, "We want people to think of us as the Nordstrom of plumbing repair," or "We want to be the Nordstrom of the insurance industry," or "We want to be known as the Nordstrom of pest control."

Regardless of the industry, every organization wants to be associated with Nordstrom's customer-centric brand promise and reputation for treating customers with legendary service. Nordstrom, across all industries, has become the benchmark to emulate.

As a Seattle native, I've always been aware that the Nordstrom clothing stores are special. If you buy something at Nordstrom and you don't like it, don't want it anymore, have decided it doesn't match the rest of your wardrobe, or have left it sitting in your closet so long that it has gone out of style, Nordstrom will take it back—no questions asked. Nordstrom will refund your purchase or give you a store credit: your choice. Don't have your receipt? They will take it back anyway. Nordstrom makes it a no-risk proposition to buy from them. They have eliminated the fear of buying anything from them. Nordstrom knows that if you are treated respectfully, you will come back.

The interesting thing for me is that their "formula" is brilliantly simple, yet almost everyone who tries to "be Nordstrom" gets it wrong. Well, now you're going to hear the secrets from one of the horses' mouths. The architect for Nordstrom's explosive growth for the past four decades was Bruce Nordstrom, a third-generation Nordstrom. Bruce took over the company in 1963, and while he ran the place, the company grew from an annual volume of $40 million to $3 billion by 1990. From 1978 to 1998, the stock split six times.

So how does a company founded in 1901 remain so relevant? Well, I was thrilled to pose that question to Bruce Nordstrom. Among other things, he was excited to tell me that the fourth generation is firmly ensconced and doing spectacular business. Bill, Blake, Dan, Erik, Jim, and Pete Nordstrom—brothers and cousins, all between the ages of 31 and 34—took over the business in 1995. As Bruce Nordstrom told the *Seattle Post-Intelligencer,* "We were getting old. This is a young person's business. You have to adapt to change. You have to look at it fresh."

Ross Shafer: Your company was founded in 1901 when your grandfather, John Nordstrom, used his Alaskan "gold rush" stake to open a shoe store in downtown Seattle, correct?
Bruce Nordstrom: Yes, and then, in 1928, he sold out to his sons, Everett and Elmer. My dad, Everett, ran it for a long time, and then I took it on. As a now fourth-generation family business, we've been through a lot of changes in the last hundred years. For example,

when my uncle Elmer was running things, it was a tiny little shoe store doing about $300,000 a year. When they left in 1963, I was named president and we were doing about $40 million. Today we do a fair bit more than that.

RS: Nordstrom has such an incredible legacy of unparalleled customer service. How did that start?

BN: It's always been a part of our family culture. We all worked the floor and were taught that by our family. I remember being a young man, working in the store and having people come up to me and say, "Mr. Nordstrom, you must come from a very nice family to have generated this kind of service and the good things you do for customers. So that makes you a wonderful person, because your attention to your customers is really quite amazing." And I remember saying to myself, "Oh, no, it doesn't make me a wonderful person. I think it actually makes me greedy because that kind of treatment works!" But, you know, we didn't always behave this way. When I was young, we were much tougher on "policy," but we found that the more responsive we were to our customers, the more money they would spend with us. Quite honestly, we learned this by trial and error.

RS: It works because it's profitable. But it also puts pressure on your competitors, correct?

BN: It drives them crazy. We strive to be nicer than our competitors. You know, some of the nicest letters I've received have been from people who compliment us on the service. And we know that it raises the bar for other retailers when we go into a new market.

RS: If the formula is so simple, why don't more companies adopt it?

BN: I think they "get it" intellectually, but it's too easy to pay lip service to how you should treat customers. It's not a Band-Aid. It's a culture. We've been doing business this way for a long time, so anyone who comes to work here knows what we expect from them. New hires know that if they want to keep their job, they have to live up to that level.

RS: Has the company philosophy changed since you now have to answer to shareholders?

BN: Oh, yeah. We have been a publicly held company since 1971, and there are some who would think that giving so much money back is too liberal. And I would remind those people that that's what got us here.

RS: Since this book is about remaining relevant, how would you describe the Nordstrom philosophy regarding relevance?

BN: Well, first of all, being in the fashion industry forces you to be current. You can't wake up and say, "Well, I know it all now." You know, today we have scores of buyers, and the really good ones are innovative. They have new ideas and are always on the lookout for innovation or something special. That's kind of an obvious skill set for being a buyer. But what might surprise you is that they are vitally concerned about the point of sale. The point of sale is critical. Almost all of our competitors have buyers and store operators, and those positions are separate. They are two completely separate things—buying, and selling on the floor. But the best buyers are the ones who spend a lot of time on the sales floor with the department managers and the store managers, teaching and learning from them. That doesn't seem very innovative, except that it is: everything is new, everything is happening for the first time, and you need to experience it.

RS: Organizations always need a fresh infusion of ideas. How do you accomplish that?

BN: Every organization needs fresh blood and new ideas. I just retired as chairman of the board, and actually, my children are running this thing a hell of a lot better than I ever did. We just had our August [2007] figures come in, and we were the number-one retailer in the whole country for percentage and gain in the business. And I'm not doing a damn thing other than I'm just kind of the cheerleader around here, allowing our kids that are young, and maybe a little green—but wait. They're not so young and green anymore! They're in their mid-40s, and they've been doing this thing since they were fourteen years old. So they've got a lot of years that they've been selling shoes. You've got to have confidence to turn to a fresh face and say, "It's your responsibility, and I'm not going to get mad at you if you fail. And I'm going to give you all the credit if you win."

RS: Did this attitude come naturally to you, or did you pick this up along the way?

BN: Watching and learning. One of the things that had a huge impact on me was knowing this star manager named Harry. He was really good. And every time he got promoted, I would take over his job. The thing is, he was only twenty-one years old when my dad made him the buyer of our biggest shoe department.

RS: Twenty-one is quite young, isn't it?

BN: Right. We don't go that young for a position like that now, but the business was smaller and my dad made him the buyer—which was a huge responsibility. Well, he and my dad went back to New York to the big clothing market, and the vendors "clothing-sampled" him. And, of course, everybody goes over to my dad, who wasn't an old man at the time, you know, and they said, "Oh, Mr. Nordstrom, we're so glad to see you. Let us show you." He would just say, "This is my buyer, Harry, and he's the one who will make the purchases," and then my dad would leave. Harry has told me that, in his whole life, that was the greatest single thing anybody ever did for him. He says, "I never worked so hard in my life just to live up to that." I believe that. Not everybody is that good, but it's your job to identify people who have this kind of ability and turn them loose. Their own sense of pride and responsibility will make them rise to great heights.

RS: Speaking of spotting talent, what is your advice for interviewing prospective employees?

BN: I'm not a big interview guy. Interviews don't matter. Performance is what matters. I think interviews can be almost counterproductive and certainly misleading. You can have a guy come in your office, and he's clean-shaven and his hair's cut and his shoes are shined—but that may be the only time he's done it all year. In our company, we wash people out as initial hires pretty fast. Because once they're in here, you quickly find out who wants to work hard, who takes to it, who has the feeling for it, and all that. So you've got to be critical of those who don't.

RS: At Nordstrom, people are expected to perform right away.

BN: Oh, absolutely. They have a standard to meet, and it's basically you've got to make your draw, and your draw's a guarantee paid, and then you make a commission override over that. Well, you're costing us money if you don't get into your override. We want you to make more money. If you're below your draw, then you're not justifying your keep. And so we find out pretty quickly.

RS: But you have surprisingly low turnover, especially at the manager level.

BN: That's right. It's common in retail to have managers playing musical chairs, jumping from company to company. But not here. By the time they get here and work their way up, they get it—they're part of our culture, and they understand it.

RS: I'm going to switch gears here for a moment. When I called you, you answered your own phone. Was I given a secret special line?

BN: [*laughs*] Nope. I only have one line, and I answer it.

RS: That's very unusual in a world of voice-menu prompts.

BN: We have phone lines like everybody else, but we have live people answering the phones. If you don't, you get off on the wrong foot with a customer. It's like that in all of our stores. We want to keep it personal.

RS: What do you do to keep learning?

BN: I pay attention to the smart people who work for us. One of our managers was interviewed down in Southern California, and she was a real star. She was running all of Southern California for us, and these magazines kept interviewing her. They said, "You must be the greatest trainer in the world to get these people to perform like this." And she says, "Oh, no, the parents were the best trainers." Isn't that brilliant? Because, actually, our people only spend about two days in training, just learning how to run the register and where the door is. You know, not a lot. You learn about our business when you get to the sales floor and it's all happening around you. Then you really see it.

RS: But only two days of training? I would have thought your training was far more extensive.

BN: It is a surprise to everyone I tell. We teach them how to use the cash register, but we don't teach people how to sell. We give them product-knowledge seminars all the time about what this product is made of, how well it is made, how it fits, all that kind of stuff. But everybody's approach is different. And I've known quiet good salespeople and loud good salespeople. I've known good black salespeople and good white salespeople. Everybody's different, has a little different slant on it, and sells in a different way. It's better that way, because the sales process is coming from each person's own personal experiences. The only criticism I would have is when someone has a canned sales pitch. Customers can see right through that and it doesn't come off as authentic. We want to remain real.

RS: You have a strong mentoring program, don't you?

BN: Very much so. But again, our mentoring all takes place on the job. We want to operate under real conditions and real scenarios. It's the only thing that matters in training. We want to know how people operate under real pressure and real circumstances.

RS: How do you select your mentors?

BN: Well, it's formally assigned, but it's not dictated by me or presidents or general managers. It's done by department managers or store managers. Those are the ones who recognize that this person would be a good mentor. You aren't a good mentor just because somebody says you should be a mentor. You have to be good at your job and unselfish about helping other people. We've been very fortunate. We have some really good salespeople, and thankfully only a few who are so selfish that they wouldn't spend any of their time doing it.

RS: You also reward people for what you call "customer heroics"?

BN: Yes. When our people go above and beyond the normal sales transaction—like driving a hundred miles to deliver an item, or waiting on the curb with a freshly pressed garment so a busy customer doesn't have to walk into the store—we reward that person with recognition and cash.

RS: I know you must have a million customer-heroics stories, but have any of them become a new standard of doing business for you?

BN: I do, but if I try to recall them all, I'll probably leave out the best ones. I'll tell you one that we have become famous for. We have a store in Tyson's Corner in Washington, D.C. As you know, they have dress-up events almost every night in that town. Well, one night a senator or other luminary called us to say he didn't know how to tie his tuxedo tie. So he drove by our store, and one of our salespeople went out to his limo and tied his tie for him. Now we get a lot of people coming by for our "tuxedo tying service."

RS: Your stores are beautiful and feel very "upscale," but whose idea was it to have a live grand-piano player? It's a really nice touch.

BN: Thank you. We're doing it in over half the stores now. My cousin, John, was the one most responsible for actually getting that in motion. And the key thing he did, which we all disagreed with, was demand that all of the pianos be Steinways. The rest of us said, "What? Do you know what that would cost?" John said, "Yes, it's expensive, but we've got to do this. Steinways are the best." And he was right; he immediately elevated what we were doing in there. Everybody noticed. It's a top-notch piano played by real artists.

RS: OK, Bruce, I've saved this final note for last, because I didn't want to color the interview in any way. For the last three years, my younger son Ryan has sold shoes in your Seattle and Bellevue, Washington, stores while he's worked his way through the University of Washington. It's been a very successful and incredible experience for him.

BN: Good for him. Then he can tell you if I've been lying to you, too.

RS: You haven't. You've echoed everything he's told me about Nordstrom—except you've done it with more humility. My son brags about you.

BN: Tell him to stop by and see me sometime—or call. I answer my own phone, you know.

Blowing the Old Loyalty Formulas Out of the Water

Earning customer loyalty is easy if you know the most important truism.

As long as humans continue to buy from other humans, whether it is over the phone, in person, or online, the amount of *relevant emotionality* in the customer's experience with you is the only way you will ever get a fair shot at loyalty and repeat business. Put another way: customer/client/patient loyalty only grows when they have an *emotional* connection with you. Nothing else draws people near you like friendship—even if it is just perceived friendship.

Customer Empathy—Not Service

Customer service is dead. People don't want "service" anymore.

I had already produced several human resources training films on customer service and was looking for a fresh angle. In 2004 and 2005, we were researching customer complaints for a new book, *The Customer Shouts Back*. I wanted to know if what we knew about customers was still relevant, so I dissected one thousand random complaints that we found on open forum websites and blogs all over the planet. I mined sites such as www.complaints. com, www.my3cents.com, www.clik2complaints.com, www. thesqueakywheel.com, www.fightback.com, and www.trading-standards.co.uk. I favored this approach because there was no way our research team could interfere with the data. We weren't involved in the collection of the data. People were already disappointed with the transaction and were freely typing into cyber-space to let off steam or ask for help.

Every Transaction Is Emotional.

Every monetary transaction is about the heart.

What surprised me the most was that these customers weren't just complaining; they were on their proverbial last nerve. They had already lived through the terrorist attacks of September 11, the dot.com implosion, two Gulf wars, an eroding environment, and corporate debacles from Enron to HealthSouth. They had grown less tolerant of incompetence and had specific *feelings* associated with bad customer service. When a customer wasn't smiled at, they *felt disliked*. If a sales associate didn't make eye contact, they *felt unimportant*. When a customer wasn't acknowledged, they *felt rejected*. If a clerk used foul language within earshot of the customer, the customer *felt embarrassed, insulted,* and often *angry*.

Apparently, they felt a certain amount of anonymity by typing over the Internet, because they wrote freely about feeling vulnerable, anxious, out of control, and helpless. This was a revelation to an old training dog like me. This behavioral shift hit me like a stone in the throat. The customers weren't always right. In this complex world, they are now the vulnerable buyers. The customers don't have all the answers, so they're looking to you for help. You are the expert. The truth is that they need you, and they don't like needing you. Compare this to your own personal relationships. Have you ever been in a romantic relationship where you loved the other person more than he or she loved you? You become the vulnerable party who asks, "You aren't going to hurt me, are you?" That is exactly how your clients and customers feel. Why? Because we humans only have one emotional barometer for how we interpret and respond to pain and pleasure.

Walk in the Vulnerable Customer's Shoes

Everybody is vulnerable because we don't know *your* business.

Imagine how vulnerable you might feel if you were buying a new house and had to sit down to sign a two-inch-tall stack of unfamiliar legal papers. You wouldn't be very comfortable, would you? Do you read every word of the molecule-sized print? Unless you read these papers every day of your life, you have to trust your mortgage lender and realtor to watch your backside.

How vulnerable would you feel if you discovered you were overdrawn at the bank and you realized that it was probably your fault? How would you feel if you had to go into the bank branch to cover the shortage? Most customers in that situation said they felt embarrassed and humiliated.

How vulnerable would you feel if an auto mechanic told you the broken motor mount will cost $1,200? Do you know if he's right? Are you a car expert, or do you have to trust the mechanic?

Pretty easy to see how *you* could feel anxious and helpless, right?

You can eliminate your customers' vulnerability with kindness and empathy. Try to understand how they feel during this transaction. When your customers and clients feel loved by you, they feel tremendous relief. Now they can stop "dating" other companies.

Every Company Can Spike Revenues
When You Spot Vulnerability

Everyone in our family rides motorcycles.

It doesn't matter if you ride a Harley, Honda, Suzuki, Ducati, or Kawasaki. The brand doesn't matter. We all just love riding together. We love the open road and stopping for lunch at any shabby café.

One day my father-in-law, Lee, opened his garage to find his battery dead. This is the worst sunny-day disappointment of every rider. Lee removed the battery and took it to a local Honda shop for a charge. A couple hours later, he took the battery back home— about 30 miles—only to realize that the nuts weren't on the battery posts, and he couldn't install the wires without them. Lee called the shop, and they offered to drive to his home to return the nuts.

Talk about customer empathy!

Battery cables firmly in place, Lee got to take a ride. And because the mechanic empathized with Lee's frustration, and made an inconvenient trip to satisfy him, Lee will shop with them forever.

Empathy When Eating Alone

If you want to see one of the best examples of customer empathy in action, visit any one of the more than seventy McCormick & Schmick's seafood restaurants.

Business-wise, they have had twenty consecutive quarters of sales growth. Beyond the impressive numbers, if you like great seafood, this will be a treat for you. They offer more than thirty different kinds of fresh seafood. In fact, the food is so fresh that the menu has to be printed twice daily. The bar only serves cocktails made with fresh fruit. No blended drinks. Yes, they've got the food and beverage components nailed! But their business continues to flourish because their extraordinary menu is accompanied by skilled, personal service. They do more than explain dish preparation; the chef graces your table personally to make your mouth water. If you are dining alone in one of their restaurants, the server will ask you, "Can I get you a newspaper or reading glasses to help pass the time?" They always make a point of learning your name and asking how you heard about them. In the past three years, I've probably eaten in sixteen of their restaurants, and I've always had a memorable experience. Reliability, consistency, and empathy are relevant traits.

Speaking of Food ...

Another restaurant chain that impresses with their relevance is Boston's/Boston Pizza company.

George Melville and Jim Treliving bought this small franchise operation in 1983, and have since built the chain to more than two hundred stores. Their growth has been phenomenal because they are obsessed with every small step of the customer experience. They have a very specific experience planned for you that starts in the parking lot. Boston's knows that the positive way you feel after you have paid the check is the emotion that will bring you back.

At an international franchisee conference, I heard Boston Pizza International's president, Mark Pacinda, enthusiastically describe the total customer experience this way:

> The experience begins the moment your guests approach your front door. The door opens for them, and your guests are surprised and delighted to be met by a greeter who welcomes them warmly and leads them immediately to their table. Your guests can't help but notice that their table is spotless and

perfectly set. They look around and the whole restaurant is immaculate, and that just adds to their
growing feeling of comfort.

Just as quickly as they settle, their cheerful
server arrives to take their drink orders and offer
assistance with their menu choices. That server is
not only going to answer any question they might
have, but also invite them to try an add-on or
participate in a special promotion, all the while
building their anticipation of the delicious food
that will soon be arriving.

When those meals arrive, the timing is perfect,
and the fresh, hot meal is exquisitely prepared and
masterfully presented.

"My God, it looks just like it does in the menu!"
Their eyes widen at the sight of this wonderful food, their nostrils fill with the tantalizing
aromas, and then they take a bite. Perfection.
And as they make their way to their car, across
your neatly maintained parking lot, they argue.
Yeah, argue—about whose idea it was to come to
Boston Pizza in the first place. They all want to
take the credit.

Boston's is a company that is obsessed with the customer's
emotional experience. Every step of the way, the restaurant
management and staff are thinking about the *customer's* perspective, not their own. They are so concerned about providing the total customer experience before, during, and after the
transaction that they can't help but keep growing the franchise
at a record pace.

Are "Frequent Purchase"
Cards a Relevant Customer Experience?

No, but you should offer a "frequent purchase" card because everybody else has them. It's a given if you want to appear competitive.

Loyalty cards were an outgrowth of the airline industry's frequent-flyer miles. Frequent patronage entitled the customer to free flights. Retailers picked up on the idea to offer special discounts for repeat business. In fact, the discount is more of a perceived discount. But is that relevant?

Darrel Zahorsky of About.com says:

> Actually, it's something that companies need to do, but it's just a cost of doing business now. You almost need to have them. But because everybody else has it, these cards are no longer a competitive advantage. It's not really relevant to loyalty. It's more of an expectation of business; there are just so many loyalty cards out there. My wallet has, like, fourteen, fifteen cards in it, and I don't feel any more loyal to the company. I just feel it's rewarding me by giving me a discount. Companies need to understand what loyalty really is. It's an emotional "something" you can't buy. You have to earn it.

Relevant Review

Empathy matters. Service does not.

A culture of customer *empathy* feels far different to people because it's emotional. Empathy means you are attempting to understand the customers' emotional state before, during, and after your interaction with them. Service is merely transactional and doesn't necessarily invoke an emotional reaction.

Loyalty can only occur by establishing a caring and respectful relationship. Does this have to be a human-to-human, talking-listening relationship, or can you create that feeling and experience online?

Direct human communication is faster, because trust and rapport happens faster in person or over the telephone. We talk. They listen. We complain. They solve the problem. The outgrowth is trust and a desire to be treated well—again.

However, of all the online experiences, Amazon.com comes the closest to creating loyalty by creating trust through reliability, responsiveness, and choice. They respect their customers and never let them down. If there is a complaint or misstep, it is handled immediately to the customer's delightful resolution. Zappos, the online shoe retailer, combines the Amazon online reliability with the human-voice touch. Later in this book, I'll profile their exponential growth due to some of these factors.

What can you do to show your clients, customers, and patients that you care about them as people? What can you do to take the emphasis away from you and show more empathy toward the people who are paying your bills and growing your company? Are you respecting their complaints? Are you giving them what they continually ask for? Do you take into consideration how they *feel* as they go through the sales transaction with you?

If not, why not?

Does your competition do a better job of this than you do?

Chapter 8

Like It or Not, Everybody Sells

Don't Call Me a Salesperson

Everyone sells: the security team, the receptionists, the payroll clerk, the legal team, the stock room team—and everyone else.

Everyone.

I often work with back-office support teams who vehemently deny they operate in a sales role. They don't like the term "salesperson," and they certainly don't want to be thought of that way.

Sad to say, you don't get to vote. Your clients and customers view everyone in your organization as a salesperson. Whether you work in the shipping department, the accounts payable department, the parts division, or the trucking crew, your actions either enhance or degrade the way your company is perceived by a client or customer. *Everyone* in your organization is in "sales."

(If I repeat this enough, you might believe me).

Remember the "lost-motorcycle-battery-nuts" story in the previous chapter? If this were a three-act Broadway play, act 1 would start by showing us that our protagonist (Lee) has a conflict (dead battery). This sets up the scenario for one of the lead characters (Mr. Mechanic) to come to the rescue.

In act 2, our protagonist Lee feels beholden to Mr. Mechanic, so he looks for a reason to repay the favor. In this case, Mr. Mechanic's kindness will provoke a potentially profitable effect. The dead battery made our protagonist think it might be time to buy a new motorcycle. He was so impressed by the empathy of Mr. Mechanic that after Lee sold his bike the following weekend, his first stop was Mr. Mechanic's company, from whom he decided to buy a new motorcycle from.

Amongst all of the gleaming motorcycles on the sales floor, Lee falls in love with one particular bike. But he's a due-diligence buyer. He wants to compare it against one at another shop down the road. At 4:00 PM, one of Mr. Mechanic's salespeople gives him a firm quote on the bike, and Lee tells the salesperson, "I'd like to sleep on it."

Act Three begins. By 9:00 AM the next day, Lee has made his decision. So he treks back to the store, sees that his motorcycle of choice is still there, and tells a *different* salesperson he'd like to buy it. Lee is told that the bike *he* wanted was sold last night and that an exact replica has been parked in its place. Worse, the "new" bike costs $1,000 more than the one that was sitting there yesterday. Lee knows the salesperson is lying because he recognizes the exact bike he'd looked at the day before. It had the same exact markings and options—but is missing the price tag.

After a few argumentative words, Lee waves his checkbook in the salesperson's face and marches out of the shop to buy from another dealer. Sadly, the experience had an associative effect on the sale as well. Lee ended up buying an entirely different brand.

The point is that everyone in your organization has tremendous sales power. While the parts guy did not think of himself as a salesman, his actions convinced a qualified buyer to return for a much larger purchase. Your personality and kind actions make customers and clients feel good about your organization. That's "salesmanship"—whether or not you like to think of it that way.

But If You Don't "Ask for the Sale," You're Not a Salesperson, Right?

Wrong. A researcher at one of the "Top Four" investment brokerage firms told me about an interesting study they had done. The study was based on the question, "What percentage of our happy clients with $500K investment portfolios would refer us to a friend?" The answer was a staggering 88 percent. That number didn't surprise me.

It makes sense. If you are happy with your stockbroker, why wouldn't you refer that broker to your friend? You will look like a hero to your friend. Every investor is anxious to learn about a broker who can grow their money faster.

The answer to the second question in the survey was even more enlightening: "What percentage of our brokers purposefully asks for a referral?" Sadly, only 11 percent of the stockbrokers bothered to ask their clients for referrals. They didn't ask because they didn't want to be accused of being a "salesperson."

This is flawed thinking.

If you aren't asking for the business, you are doing your clients a disservice. If you are good at what you do, your clients want you to ask. They want to help you. That's not salesmanship. It is telling your friends about something that will benefit them.

Haven't We Heard Enough About "Relationship" Selling?

Never. Good relationships create strong emotional connections. Emotional connections spawn loyalty. Loyalty causes people to buy from you even when your price is higher and your orders are late.

Relationship selling is what every customer wants, and it has nothing to do with your sales technique. Your clients and customers have seen enough reality TV to know what's fake and what isn't. They want you to be honest and authentic. A relationship, from their perspective, is showing an interest in their lives. They want a connection with you that doesn't always revolve around business.

Here's a Horror Story for You

I met a financial planner at a banking conference who told me about one of his most devastating client blunders:

> I had this client, a quiet sort of guy who owned a print shop in town. His portfolio with me was about $700,000, which was nice, but not one of my bigger fish. One day I hear from a mutual friend that he sold his print shop to a major chain for $16 million. I had no idea his little shop was worth that kind of money. So I call the guy to make an appointment about investing. He says, "I don't know what I'm going to do. It's almost Christmas, and I may splurge and buy something fun for myself." So, I backed off. In January, I call again and find out from his wife that the man died just after Christmas. I explained to his wife that I was their stockbroker. She interrupts me to say, "I don't know you. I've never met

you. You've never been to our house. I'm going to let our son handle our finances."

The financial planner really blew it. If he had taken the time and effort to create a relationship with the man and his family, rather than just servicing the portfolio, he could have become the family's trusted advisor. He would have been perfectly positioned to maintain and grow the account. He might even have been in line to be referred to the widow's friends. Instead, he was shut down because he didn't show an interest in creating a relationship.

Roger Staubach's Sales Team Thrives on Integrity

If you're a diehard football fan, you've heard the name "Roger Staubach." If you aren't, you'll love this American success story anyway.

In the 1970s, Roger Staubach was the prototype of the precision quarterback. Staubach was instrumental in helping the Dallas Cowboys become "America's Team." He guided them through nine of their record-setting twenty consecutive winning seasons. Staubach helped lead the Cowboys to their first Super Bowl victory, and as a result, he was named MVP in Super Bowl IV. Staubach was described by his legendary coach Tom Landry as "possibly the best combination of a passer, an athlete, and a leader to ever play in the NFL."

His success started with a pedigree of character.

His path to NFL stardom began in college when he was a quarterback for the U.S. Naval Academy. Staubach won the Heisman Trophy in 1963, and was a tenth-round draft pick of the Dallas Cowboys in the 1964 NFL draft. However, because of his military commitment, Staubach did not begin playing pro ball until 1969. While most ballplayers would be anxious to launch a career in the NFL, Roger signed up for a tour of Vietnam. He entered the NFL as a twenty-seven-year-old rookie. That should give you a window into Staubach's character.

The Quarterback Mogul

After his Hall-of-Fame football career, Staubach went into the real estate business—but in a very unusual way. Typically, if you own commercial real estate, you enlist a commercial real estate agent to represent you in lease agreements. But Staubach noticed that nobody was representing the tenants. It was a revolutionary idea.

Today, The Staubach Company is a multibillion-dollar commercial real estate brokerage firm headquartered in Dallas, Texas. The firm has more than seventy offices, and is part of a worldwide partnership with DTZ, a British commercial real estate firm.

I thought Roger Staubach would be the perfect person to talk about growth and how he evaluates his highly productive sales staff.

Ross Shafer: Roger, you have experienced exponential growth since you opened your doors in 1981, and the people I've talked to say you have grown your brand on a foundation of integrity and honesty.

Roger T. Staubach: Thank you. It's really worked out for us.

RS: I've heard you say that if people trust you in one area—say, your personal life—that they're going to trust you in another area. This has been a hallmark of your life, and you look for that in your sales staff, correct?

RTS: Well, that's what you should be able to do. I think you have to try to be consistent in what you do all the time. And I mean in your personal and business life. We're all a little quirky. But you will undermine your credibility if you have a pattern of behavior that is totally inconsistent in one area compared to another area, especially where you're trying to send a business message of total integrity.

RS: I have a friend who left a big Wall Street firm and is writing a book about ethics and deceit on Wall Street. He claims when you're around "morally flexible" behavior every day, and everybody's doing it, you become convinced that because everyone else is doing it, it must not be so bad.

RTS: That's exactly right. It's so easy to rationalize everything you do. It's kind of strange to see how companies and executives can almost compartmentalize their behavior.

RS: Isn't it easier to maintain a standard when you have boundaries set up for honesty and integrity? If you want a culture of integrity, isn't it best to be crystal clear: "This is what we expect and this is how we do things here"?

RTS: That's right. And people are constantly looking to see you compromise your principles ... for *them*. But if integrity is who you are and what you want to be, it's not hard to live those principles. It's when you're putting principles up there and not following them—that's when you really get screwed up. Your behavior in the company has got to be consistent across your personal life, too. I think that's important in an organization. Sometimes you can get away without it because you're so driven, as far as being a business person, but your people want to look at you with respect. If you're preaching this message, they want to see it in practice.

RS: What about the inadvertent mistakes or the misunderstandings?

RTS: There are still things that happen where your people don't understand all the circumstances on why decisions are made. But I will do everything I can to clarify why we do things, because I want them to feel good about being with us. With fourteen hundred people here, I just want every one of them to be happy and pleased.

RS: How do you weed out the "bad eggs?"

RTS: There's always going to be the "bad quirkies" who are going to be in your mix. But we find them pretty quickly, and they're not the ones making decisions or representing the company. If you look at the client review form, it pops up, sure enough. Something goes wrong, and, in most of the cases, if there have been some issues with that person, we correct it.

RS: You encourage good people to make decisions in the interest of the customer.

RTS: We have some wonderful examples of negotiating on behalf of the customer in which our salespeople make smaller commissions, but it's the right thing to do for the customer. And they *should* do that, because that's where the trust is. In our business, you'll really get caught up in the middle of a lot of transactions with your customer in which they just trust you're leading them in the right direction— and technology aside, the human factor is involved in every business. We never forget the human side of the business. You've got to be able to get that kind of feeling and that kind of spirit in your company, whether you're a large company or a small company, because everyone will transfer that spirit to the customer.

RS: What kind of hiring metric do you use to find the right people for your company?

RTS: Because most of our team is sales-driven, we have this caliber testing that's just been phenomenal for us. It's not hiring by the seat of your pants, or having someone who refers a friend to us. There is much more to it than that. A lot of things go into our hiring—and it's working, because our retention has been better than it's ever been. We've been getting better at hiring the right people and putting them in the right jobs. Sometimes you hire the right people, but you put them in the wrong jobs.

RS: Are you looking for a certain personality type?

RTS: In a sense, yes. I'll give you an example. We had a couple of folks we hired, and they were really great people, but they just couldn't make calls. We had them in a sales role where they're going out to get business, and there are just some people who can't do that—which shows us that it's a pretty neat testing program. It's more based on the person rather than on what their strengths are. It is not a test to see how smart you are.

RS: Ultimately, you're also doing the right thing by the employee.

RTS: I really believe, to be relevant, you've got to really show an appreciation for the work that's done by the people in your organization. A lot of different people touch the customer. In our case, we've got staff people who are paid a lot less than brokers who are out there getting big commissions, but the reason we got return business from the customer was because of the work done by *every* person who was servicing the customer. So we appreciate everyone who works here.

RS: How do you show your appreciation?

RTS: We consistently acknowledge hard work. We thank people and we honor people by trying not to have big shots with big offices.

RS: It is easy to tell from this conversation that you promote a culture of humility.

RTS: I'm in total agreement with that. If you aren't humble, you are not going to convey that to the customer. I am on several boards—American Airlines, for example—where we always hear that the shareholders are our number-one responsibility. That's true. They are. But it's a combination that includes the shareholders and people who work for us and our customers—everyone is important. The shareholders aren't going to be pleased if we're not treating our customers properly, and our customers aren't going to be pleased if they come in contact with moody employees.

RS: Another example of your attitude toward the synergy of teamwork.

RTS: At the end of the day, we want to be in this thing together. I wouldn't run a company if I couldn't make sure that we have a big picture in mind and we want to be successful together, now. And how people are treated is critical to get to that point. I want to work with people I trust. I mentioned the "bad-quirky" people earlier. Their agendas are always designed to work for their best interests.

I don't think you can trust people like that.

RS: Are there enough "good-quirky" people to go around?

RTS: I think most people are good-quirky. You can trust good-quirky people. They want to take care of life, they want to take care of themselves, and they have responsibilities to their families. But at the same time, they also know that they have responsibilities to other people, and they can't be successful without the help of someone else. They have a better balance of their lives. They're going to weigh things properly, make the right decisions, and keep *your* interests at heart, too—not just their own.

In a Recession, Hire More Salespeople.

Don't get cheap during a recession.

When most companies are squeezing the blood from nickels and pinching pennies, the idea of hiring more salespeople may sound counterintuitive. But listen to the logic of Mark McComb, chief operating officer of SelectRemedy Staffing. McComb has been with the company for sixteen years, and has watched it grow from a single small office to the $1 billion industry leader in employee staffing.

Ross Shafer: In sixteen years you've been through a few different business cycles. You have also grown through key acquisitions as well as organically. Was this a thought-out plan or the result of serendipitous opportunities?

Mark McComb: Both—but there has always been a steadfast plan for organic growth. One thing that we have always focused on is sales. We combat recessions by hiring more sales representatives. Where our competition will lay off their sales representatives, or change their compensation plans, we keep hiring and paying our people well. And that's not to say that we don't tighten the belt or that we don't have high expectations of production during a downturn. But it has always been our culture to sell through tough times and notice opportunities to gain some market share while others are backing off.

RS: Your sales team also remains relevant by offering innovative services—services that might be expensive, especially when others are tightening their belts.

MM: Right. One of those services is being able to provide cost information to our clients. We want our clients to use that information to measure productivity online. It gives them peace of mind.

RS: Does that apply to your temp-to-permanent workers, or is it across the board?

MM: It's across the board, from temps to high-level executives. We are doing a lot more consultation with our high-volume clients regarding how they could schedule their shifts a little differently, or work in incentives, compensation—the sorts of things that will deliver more return on their staffing dollar.

RS: The "trusted advisor" concept instead of just being a staffing vendor.

MM: That's what we do. It's our edge. And the advantage for our clients is that we work with thousands of companies, so we are exposed to a plethora of best practices. Our clients love that we are able to take these best practices and apply them to new companies and situations.

The SelectRemedy lesson is clear. When economic times get tight, don't pull in the horns that generate your greatest revenue. Your competition will do that and end up neglecting their clients. They will stand by and watch their market share diminish. Take a proactive approach. Offer more services. Engage more clients and customers as a trusted advisor and not as a *supplier* or *vendor*. Vendors can only compete on price. Trusted advisors compete on experience and expertise—never money.

Relevant Review

Everybody in your organization is a salesperson, whether or not they think of themselves that way. Everyone is in a position to tell your company story and reflect your company values and brand. Are they representing you well? Are they behaving in ways that would encourage people to buy from you—or better yet, to come to work for you?

Sales isn't just bobbing and weaving to wiggle money out of people. Sales is an attitude, from the way the receptionist answers the phone to the way the security guard treats visitors to the way the service department discusses a technical issue to the way a payroll clerk hands you your paycheck. It is a powerful, company-wide attitude that says (without saying): "I like what we do here, and I'm proud of what we sell. We can solve your problems in a way that will make you glad you chose to spend your money here."

Oh yes—and *everybody* sells.

Chapter 9

How Can You Be Relevant in the Global Market?

Luckily, We Can Learn from Bob Walsh

Who the Hell Is Bob?

That is the title of a book documenting one of the most incredible careers anyone could dream of. His résumé sounds unbelievable, but it is all true.

Bob Walsh

- is credited with creating "March Madness" for NCAA College Basketball;
- co-created and produced the Goodwill Games with Ted Turner;
- managed the Seattle Supersonics NBA basketball team;
- launched the nickname "Emerald City" for Seattle when

nobody thought it would ever catch on;
- created the first NBA franchise in Canada;
- managed more than one hundred professional athletes in twelve different sports;
- launched a rocket from the former Soviet Union to the United States against the wishes of NASA;
- has pharmaceutical products named after him in nine countries;
- won a landslide lawsuit against the U.S. Olympic Committee when they tried to block him from pursuing Seattle as a site for the 2012 Olympic Games.

Though just five feet four inches tall, by any measure Bob Walsh is a dynamo who has taken the world by storm. Walsh learned a savvy lesson about salesmanship when he and media mogul Ted Turner wanted to create and produce the Goodwill Games—an Olympic-level athletic competition designed to heal the Cold-War wounds between the Soviet Union and the United States. But history made this a difficult task

The 1979 invasion of Afghanistan caused the United States and other Western countries to boycott the 1980 Summer Olympics in Moscow, an act reciprocated when the Soviet and other Eastern-Bloc countries boycotted the 1984 Summer Olympics in Los Angeles.

Although Bob and Ted's excellent adventure was to sell the Russians on the idea of a jointly sponsored world event, Walsh quickly learned that "selling" had nothing to do with the equation.

It was all about trust.

Naturally, all selling is about trust; but how do you pull that off in a previously hostile culture? Walsh would discover that, in Russia, trust is won through the consumption of vodka ... lots and lots of vodka. Vodka is the social and business lubricant that bonds people in those countries. So, every business meeting started with passing the bottle, laughing, sharing stories, and maybe some business. Walsh told me, "The business usually took place days or weeks after the drinking." If Walsh had sat down and tried to hammer out a deal before getting sloshed, he would have been thrown out of the country. The old saying, "When in Rome," also applied to Leningrad (now St. Petersburg—again). As a result, the Russians never thought of Bob as a salesman. He was a comrade. And because they had so much trust in Bob, they offered him real-estate development deals, pharmaceutical-company partnerships, and even a wine distributorship.

I cornered Walsh for an interview to get his perspective on how to be effective on the global stage:

Ross Shafer: So many organizations are interested in how to succeed and be relevant in a global market, and you've done that. You have great experiences to pass on to American companies who want to do business in a foreign land. Your vodka stories are legendary. I'm afraid I wouldn't have lasted very long in those negotiations.

Bob Walsh: I didn't! At my size, I could only give it my best shot and hope to survive the next day. But to answer your question, you know, the thing that really impressed me the most was a statement Ted Turner evoked—it actually became a policy that he used with everyone at CNN—which was that we were forbidden to use the word "foreigner." He wanted everyone to realize, "We're all foreigners. If you go to Iraq, we're foreigners. If you go to Iran, we're foreigners. Until they come here, they're foreigners." He said, "When you say someone is a foreigner, it sounds like they're from another world or another planet or something, and we're all people on the earth. Never think of other people as foreigners." I thought was a pretty good way to start a respectful relationship. So when we went over to the Soviet Union to talk to them about the first Goodwill Games, I always tried to think of people as just people. They're just from a different geographical location than we are, and they have different cultures and everything. But let's think of them as people on the same level, and treat them as though they know as much as we do—which they do. Because we started on that footing, we never had problems over there.

RS: This was during a time when the Cold War was ending and Mikhail Gorbachev was promoting glasnost. It was a fragile time for our two countries.

BW: Yes, which is why I found this approach to be so profound. When you're dealing with the former Soviet Union or the Eastern-Bloc countries, it can be a real trap over there unless you have their trust. If you have their support and they think of you as someone who doesn't have an agenda to rip them off, you will be dealt with fairly and cooperatively. In all the years we dealt with the different countries and the former Soviet Union, we never had one single problem of people trying to steal money from us under the table.

RS: So how do you establish the trust?

BW: I always go back to humanity first. Get to know and work with them; don't immediately try to put a business over there. We did a lot of humanitarian activities—things to support them and help them—before we tried to do business with them.

RS: Like what?

BW: Well, there was no system to help handicapped people. No buses. People would be living in small apartments, but they had no elevators. They couldn't get out of their homes. So we worked with some of the city officials to get them to do that. We brought children from their country to the United States for medical treatment. So when it came time to do business with them, we already had all these positive experiences as proof that we cared about people. We had that reputation, not only over there, but in other parts of the world as well.

RS: Bob, this is an example of extreme networking. You and I have talked about one of the best ways to network with people: when you meet with them, first ask what you can do for them.

BW: Yes. Absolutely.

RS: And that's what you were doing. You were exercising that principle without an agenda. Consequently, they had no sense of reciprocal obligation from you?

BW: No. If you don't expect something in return, the return is always bigger than you could imagine. But I have to tell you, I've made that mistake in my life. Sometimes I would think, "Well, I did something for that person. How come they're not doing something for me in return?" That's a big mistake.

RS: OK, aside from philanthropy, if you were to give advice to organizations now who are dealing with India and China and Korea, what would you tell them?

BW: The first thing, obviously, is to learn their culture and learn their language. We had a lot of people who did that working for us. They respect you so much more if you speak their language, even if you speak just a little bit.

RS: I notice that traveling abroad.

BW: That's a big thing. Americans are arrogant about our language. English is spoken just about everywhere, but if you take the time to learn Chinese or Arabic, or any language that you're going to be working in, you'll be respected more because you took the time to learn the language. Secondly, you need to learn the culture. You need to learn the history. You can't go into those countries and work with people from another country and not know about it. I've seen that hurt a lot of people in business.

RS: I have a friend at the Gallup organization who says that "you can't walk into a foreign country with your seven American rules for customer service, because you're denigrating what they do and how they do it."

BW: Right.

RS: How do you get to know the culture within the parameters of you trying to make money?

BW: I think it's very important to find some people who are either from that country or who have lived in that country, and who have taken the time to get some experience and understand the culture.

For example, I think Starbucks has done a great job of that. They go into a new country, and the first thing they do is search around and find a good partner from that country. So that partner has a real stake in it, and they're from there. And because they're Indian, or Chinese, or Korean, or Russian—whatever nationality they happen to be—they already know the customs and mores. We always found good partners, and that's what Starbucks does. They have really good partners. They don't have franchises; they have partners.

RS: Makes sense. How did you find reputable partners?

BW: When we worked in Georgia (formerly a part of the Soviet Union), we went straight to the ambassadors. We went to old, old friends whom I'd worked with over there in the '80s, and we came up with the best partners we could find. They were people we could really trust, and they represented us on the ground over there. You need to find somebody to represent you on the ground. The next thing you need to do is to put some people from your company over there with them so you know what's actually going on. You need to have several people living there, like expatriates, who are looking out for your interests. There is another key lesson I've learned: don't try to impress them with the fact that you're an American and that *they* have got to behave like Americans, or that you have a big house and *they* should have a big house, too. It's the worst thing you can possibly do.

RS: Can you talk about the American companies who are seizing what they think of as the so-called "China Opportunity"? Many American businesses think, "Wow, this is a great big country, and we can employ cheap labor, and we're smarter, and we're way ahead, and we're doing them a big favor by offering them these jobs." But from what you're describing, that attitude could blow up in your face.

BW: It will blow up in your face, and it happens very often to companies—big ones, like Weyerhaeuser. Several others went over there and they didn't make it because they had this attitude that "we know what we're doing, and you need to be like us." I'll give you a good example. This is a religious faux pas. The Russians, and everybody over there, embraces the Russian Orthodox religion. They weren't allowed to practice that for years and years and years. They couldn't go to a church. The government would arrest priests. When, all of a sudden, the Iron Curtain came down, American Christians with good intentions tried to push a different religion on them. It backfired so much that the government had to pass a law to keep the other religions from advertising over there. And the reason was basically not so much that they didn't want to learn about it, but because for so many years, they weren't allowed to practice their own religion: Russian Orthodox. Then all of a sudden they're being told they ought to do something else. It became a terrible situation.

RS: What should have been done instead?

BW: American Christians should have gone in slower and not jumped so hard on it like they did. I think the same is true with any business. If you go in and tell them everything they need to do is better *your* way, as if it is the right way, they are likely to reject it. Imagine going into China and telling them how to run their Starbucks. Of course, you give them the basics: how to set up a store, display the logo, etc. But maybe they don't like the same kind of coffee we like. Maybe they don't like certain pastries we sell here. Let them sell what they know will sell. It's the same thing with Germany or Italy or Russia or China or Korea when you try to tell those folks how they should run something. It just doesn't work. You really need to study. You really need to find out what the customs are.

RS: I want to jump back to something you said a moment ago. "Telling them about your big house is the worst thing you can do." What do you mean by that?

BW: We brought some people into Seattle from Eastern Europe. This was in the '80s when we were putting together the first Goodwill Games. One of the local board members, this guy who I'll call "Deke," was a very successful builder. He'd made a lot of money and he owned this huge home on Lake Washington. He had this idea—and I tried to warn him about this—to take these people on a tour of the area in his big helicopter and fly them over his house. I mean, this house had twenty-five rooms in it, and a swimming pool, etc. That's the worst thing you can do to those people who live over there because they think it's a waste. They think you should just have enough room to live in a flat or an apartment. You don't need a big house. It's showing off and demonstrating you aren't using good sense. It's a huge turnoff to them. You're telling them "You should live like this. Here I am. Look at this big, beautiful home I have."

When you go into a home in Eastern Europe, which are generally flats or apartments, they're beautiful. They have all these wonderful antiques and paintings. But they consist of a bedroom, living room, and a kitchen. That is how they live, regardless of how much money they acquire. So you just don't tell them about the excess you enjoy. You don't tell them you've got three cars. You won't impress them. You'll do the opposite. The same is true in China.

Humility is always the best approach to trust, relationships, and ongoing business strength. The best sales lesson anyone can ever learn is not to *sell* anything; rather, become a trusted advisor and friend before you try to do business with them.

Being Internationally Relevant Is Tricky

Not all great franchise ideas translate.

NordicTrack was already very well-known as the premier ski training brand of exercise equipment in the United States. But when the company wanted to expand into Canada, they assumed the Canadian market was similar.

Wrong.

First of all, direct sales—or direct-response copy and mail-order sales—just weren't a big thing in Canada like here in the States. There is a very small penetration of people who use mail order. They needed to go to the retail store. There again, the company misjudged the market. They wanted to promote a new model and new brand for all of the international stores. The brand was called Nordic Sport. Basically, it was a more high-tech machine made of graphite. You got the same workout, but it just looked updated. Sadly, it was unsuccessful, especially in the Canadian market, because people were familiar with the wooden NordicTrack. Often there would be a problem with salespeople saying, "This is NordicTrack," and people not believing them, even though the sales tag said, "Nordic Sport by NordicTrack."

Here comes the small innovation. Once they placed a wooden NordicTrack model in retail stores, the sales for the graphite product went through the roof. People were familiar with the brand, but they needed the original model next to the new one to make the brand connection.

Another issue was the sticker that said, "Made in America." While America makes great products, Canadians wanted to support the Canadian market. So they removed the "Made in America" sign and made a stronger, more relevant connection with the Canadian customer.

Subtle differences are crucial to your success. In all three cases above, a very small, culturally motivated adjustment made for an innovative sales driver.

Relevant Review

Going *global* isn't simply a decision to start offering your goods and services in another country. It's about understanding and respecting local customs and mores. It's about partnering with the right people who can help you navigate potentially dangerous waters. Just because you "got it right" in Omaha doesn't mean you can replicate your success in Beijing. Bob Walsh makes a strong point to approach global expansion with philanthropy and respect in mind first. Gain their trust and friendship before you start counting your profits.

Little gestures matter.

You've no doubt heard that you should make an attempt to speak the local language—even if you do so badly—as a sign of respect. I spoke to the Choice Hotel Group, whose brands include Comfort Inn and Radisson. Even though the international meeting was held in the United States, there was a large contingent of East Indian owners and managers in the audience. A few moments before I went onstage, I was advised to not only say "Hello" to the audience, but also "Namaste," which is an East Indian greeting meaning, "the light within me bows to the light within you."

When I used both greetings, I could see a smiling shift in the audience immediately. That genuine gesture endeared me to a large section of the audience that may have felt a tad bit slighted had I not acknowledged them in that way.

What can you do to show respect for your offshore partners? Have you taken the time to make friends before making business associates?

Chapter 10

Stop Losing Sleep Over Technology

"Hey, We Need More (and Better) Tech!"

Technology isn't a guarantee of survival.

If you have email, a website, a web store, a blog or forum, and a reliable server, you are doing your best. Sadly, we are conditioned to think that we need more, better, updated, leading-edge technology to succeed. Some companies even mistake ramping up technology for remaining relevant.

What people *really* consider relevant is personal contact.

With the rampant proliferation of cell phones, voicemail, email, and text messaging, more and more of your customers and clients are craving human contact. They want to speak to human beings. As I've mentioned, they want a trusted relationship with you so they can stop "dating" your competition. Honestly, they could not care less what generation of routers and switchers you're running. They want you to listen to what they need, and then consult with them on their choices.

And By the Way, Old Technology Is Still Very Good

I'm about to save you a ton of money.

You don't have to have the latest early-adopter technology to be efficient and effective. CxTec is a company that is making a fortune selling one- and two-year-old technology. The question you're probably asking is, "Who would want to buy old technology?" And the answer is: organizations that want a reliable system with great routers and switchers, but that simply can't afford to invest in the most current software and support packages. CxTec will not only sell you great equipment at a huge discount, but they will support it with their own trained technicians—for a lifetime. Long after the manufacturer has stopped supporting the software, CxTec will take care of you. When you are ready to upgrade, the company will buy your old gear and set you up with near-new stuff again.

Don't you wish you'd thought of this business? What is considered "old" in your industry that you could reintroduce as new again?

Going Paperless Is a Waste of Your Time

You aren't going to become paperless, because you still use a lot of paper. If you are growing, I would go as far as to say you are using more paper this year than you did last year.

Does this upset your "green" sensibilities? Then make a pact with yourself to recycle all of the extra paper you already use.

Face this fact: paper isn't going away soon.

Remember how we were told that the computer would enable us

to get rid of all that paper? That computer disks would eliminate the need to store paper copies in endless rows of tall filing cabinets?

It was a lie.

In *The Myth of the Paperless Office*, authors Abigail J. Sellen and Richard H.R. Harper alert us to the fact that email and the computer have actually caused us to use 40 percent *more* paper. In the old days, documents were printed, then distributed. Now, we can email the documents to many more people. They, in turn, print at their location and may distribute again. The ability to share documents digitally spelled death to the simple copy machine. As you know, the all-in-one printer can copy, scan, and print documents stored in the printer's memory, allowing you to double- and triple-task during the print process. Hewlett Packard banked everything on this evolution and built the world's largest imaging business.

The thing of it is, we like paper. We like to hold it. We like to read from it. We like to scribble notes on it. We like to write on it. It has a satisfying tactile factor that cannot be replicated on a keyboard.

We found a company who is combining the best of both paper and computer—that fits between your fingers!

Smart Pens and Smart Paper Will Make People ... Smarter

Paper and pens are going through an evolution.

Jim Margraff—one of the brains behind LeapFrog, the wonderful children's learning products company—has branched off to disrupt the tech world. His new company, Livescribe (www.livescribe.com), has created a pen-top computer. It's a pen the size of a normal fountain pen, and it writes like a normal ink pen. But this pen is anything but normal. It has an onboard camera and microphone. It also has sufficient memory to store everything being said or written.

You may not own one now, but you will before the year is out.

The Livescribe pen already is being used regularly in classrooms around the world. Corporate training centers will soon adopt them. The pen can write in your native language, then translate what you've written—in up to seventy languages! Then you can download your notes to your desktop computer.

Imagine this scenario: students can record important passages during class. Later, they can review their written and audio notes, then translate and email the notes in the languages of their study partners from different countries.

Of course, I'm only scratching the surface of the pen's capabilities. Here is Jim to describe why this technology will change the world:

Ross Shafer: Your pen has astonishing capabilities. I understand you were just invited to preview your invention at an exclusive summit of the world's top tech minds.

Jim Margraff: It was the chance of a lifetime. Walt Mossberg is a technology writer for the *Wall Street Journal*. If you Google "all things digital," you'll find information on an annual conference that he holds each year. He invites only top-tier people like Steve Jobs, Bill Gates, Steve Baumer, Peter Chernin of World News Corp, Anne Ward of *Time*, George Lucas—and this year, Eric Schmidt of Google, and the founders of YouTube. It's a real "who's who," and he brings these people up and sits them on stage and talks to them. There is no formal presentation. It's just dialogue, and anything goes. I asked him who he's having this year, and he said Jobs and Gates on stage at the same time, which just doesn't happen. He was really taken by this pen and asked me to speak at this conference. This is major league and very exciting. His comment was, "When you launch this, your product will launch a new industry." He is not a fellow who minces words. If you read his column, he is quite opinionated, and he knows what he thinks about things. He really was just taken by this.

RS: So am I! But please explain why you think paper and pen are still important, especially in a world obsessed with emerging technology.

JM: We start with basic human communication. In our society, we read, write, speak, and listen. With this pen, we can enhance those four modes of communication in a way that is quite profound. We also are linking two worlds: the paper world and the digital world. Currently, the digital linkage is modest. You do something online; you print it out. But we are allowing you to go the other way around. We can go from paper to digital, and then from digital back to paper. No one has done that. It's still a paper world, and we produce paper from those tools.

RS: I'm convinced. You're the one who told me about the book, *The Myth of the Paperless Office*.

JM: In that book, Xerox and HP offered some great studies as they looked at how paper is used and enforced in the office, what people do with it, and how people use it. In this world where you have all these tools—editing tools and graphic-design tools—why aren't we all digital? Whether you are the office worker, the consultant, the salesperson, or the designer, we all use paper. It turns out that paper is a critical part of the way that we operate. The notion of discarding paper and just moving to a digital world is something that will not happen for a long time because there are issues in convenience, access, memory, flexibility, and spatial orientation—all things that provide value to paper. So what we are doing is creating and building what I call "the paper Internet." The paper Internet is a system that links the paper to a digital world.

RS: I've seen the pen in action, but please tell the uninitiated how your pen marries paper and digital.

JM: If you had our next-generation pen in your hand right now, you would be writing your notes. As you write on the paper, it would simultaneously capture all the ink as you write and record what is being said with its two microphones. The pen would record all the audio that I'm speaking. In addition, it would link the audio to the ink on the paper as you write it. So you can go back and touch a word as you write it down—or a diagram, or any line that you drew on that paper—and you'll hear the audio that was spoken when you drew that ink.

RS: I just touch the word?

JM: Touch the word, and it will start playing the recording at that point in time when you wrote it. The technology leaders who see this realize that it is a breakthrough in the way we think about communicating. We are putting a tool in your hand that allows you to do what you do naturally: you write; people speak; you read; you listen. This tool has a lot of memory and a lot of processing power. If you had the pen in your hand right now, you would just be writing down key terms and a couple of notes. You wouldn't be scribbling, because you'd have it all recorded and you'd be able to go back and tap it to recall everything.

RS: And the cost is remarkably low, isn't it?

JM: Yes, this is extremely low-cost and powerful. Paper is the world's lowest-cost display technology, and a pen is the lowest-cost communications technology.

RS: Without any limitations to language?

JM: Yeah. The device can download context into it, so context can be created for whatever language you choose. We can actually teach you to read, to write—even in a different language—while you are speaking and listening.

RS: There is a full gigabyte of memory and a display.

JM: The display is an organic LED. It's an 18 x 96–pixel display. So you can see text, and it also scrolls—up, down, left, right. And you can navigate with it. Because of that, employee learning and training applications are exponential.

RS: There is a very successful chain of hamburger stores in the northeast called Pal's. They do all their training on iPods. Your pen could close the training loop.

JM: Yes. We have another version of this pen that is much more flexible. It provides ongoing training because, at any point in time, the student can receive more information delivered to the pen. And the information is delivered in voice or visual; you can carry on a dialogue with feedback information, and it becomes an ongoing training tool.

RS: Companies will have to adapt to these new training tools if they expect to be able to attract and retain the burgeoning Millennial workforce.

JM: We think they will. I just read an article in the *Wall Street Journal* yesterday that the big box stores have an enormous problem with turnover—shops like Home Depot, Best Buy, Kmart, Wal-Mart, and McDonald's. It's a huge problem. The big-box average employee turnover rate is at least 100 percent a year. They spend about two-and-a-half times a year's salary on recruiting, training, and keeping employees. It's just a huge burden to companies. One of the problems is the lower-cost labor force. They can't afford to bring these people in and train them, sit them down for a week and train them, because the economics aren't there. So now you've got a tool that you can put in their hand. This pen allows you to train them in the field or at home, because the low-cost tool is interactive. It provides a lot of the functionality that you had with some of our LeapPad materials, but now you have writing and speaking as well.

In addition, the corporation can now track and log the performances of people as they are being trained on paper. The workforce training implications here are incredible, and we've already discussed this with many top-brand companies. Some of the top retail corporations look at this and say, "When can we have this?!"

RS: I believe you. I want one! Can you talk about the applications beyond learning and training?

JM: First of all, there is personal productivity. There are billions of basic business forms that are filled in every year: credit card applications, sales reports expenses, customer tracking reports, relationship management, interviews, application surveys, marketing research. These forms are pervasive. Well, with this tool, when you fill in the form, the data instantly goes from the paper—wherever you are—into the back of the application. The ink can go there and it can be interpreted, and the boxes that you've checked go there, where validations can be made. So in the "form space," there's an enormous opportunity.

RS: And the corporate applications are unlimited.

JM: Corporate communications are one of our biggest challenges, as you know. Now I can write a note to somebody, and I can send it as ink or as text as I described. Or, I can jot down a few points and draw a little diagram and send it with my voice attached to it as a vocal email, so when they open their mailbox, there's a message. They click their mouse, and now they get both the few bullet points or diagram along with my voice. Or, I could sit with my paper and draw out an explanation of something, as a scientist or an engineer might want to do, and while I'm drawing it, I could explain it—and then I'll send it. Someone will receive my sketch and it will play out like a flash movie on their PC. So I can actually draw a flash movie on paper with my pen, publish it, and send it to a colleague.

RS: Professionals in science, engineering, and the construction trades could use this.

JM: Yep, architects, scientists, engineers, chemists—anyone who has to draw something to communicate it. You look at meetings where people use white boards, and they draw on a white board for a reason. It's a shared mode of communicating. This advances that concept to a whole other level. Imagine that you print out a Word document, something that someone wants you to review, and you mark it up. Wouldn't you like it to be the case that when you mark it up, those marks on the document just go right back to the author so that they get it instantly?

RS: The exciting part about this product is that it isn't limited to students, business professionals, or tradespeople. Like home computers, you're really talking about everybody owning one of these, aren't you?

JM: My goal for the next ten years is to put this into the hands of a billion people on the planet. I believe that in the future, people will have three things. You will have a communications tool, you will have a writing utensil, and you'll have a pad of paper. And those things just won't change. We are taking the writing utensil and making it an intelligent assistant that supports you and puts you online. The paper you are writing on becomes the Internet; if you want to send an email to somebody, you write it on a piece of paper. You can send it as a text, or you can send it as ink. It will arrive as an image that was drawn, or it will arrive as text. If you'd like to buy something, you'll write, "buy," and your pen will speak or display, "What do you want to buy?" You write, "Blink." It will speak or display, "A book from Malcolm Gladwell—$19.95 to purchase; please sign." And you'll sign your name on the paper, and you bought it.

RS: I have a favor to ask. In the instruction manual, can you tell your customers to order my book instead?

JM: [*laughs and mouths the word "no"*]

Honeywell Is Making Fire Alarms "Sexy?"

Today, technology has to be sexy—and easy.

Apple showed everyone in the technology sector that tech needs to have both form and function. The iPhone and iPod are runaway best sellers because of their simplicity of use and style. Cool is awesome, but making it easy to learn and user-friendly is better.

The Honeywell Life Safety division has taken a page from Apple's bible.

If you think of Honeywell as an "old-school" company, you couldn't be more wrong. I was fortunate enough to speak to several divisions of that company. Because Honeywell had devoured so many of its major competitors in the fire-safety business, I expected to see culture battles and turf wars.

Throughout my series of seminars and keynote addresses, I didn't see a single hint of a corporate skirmish. Not even a quarrel!

Instead, I saw a hard-working group of companies that are enjoying great success (even with the looming threat of a recession in the United States). I witnessed innovation, great attitudes, and intense fervor to make fire alarm equipment ... sexy.

The good feeling you get with these people is worth describing.

Because the scope of fire-alarm applications is so varied, there are many different profit centers that make up the Honeywell Life Safety division. With 7,500 employees (out of Honeywell's clan of 120,000), this group is a significant profit center for this $35 billion company. I became intimately acquainted with the fire-alarm companies: Notifier by Honeywell, Fire-Lite, Gamewell-FCI, and Silent Knight. These were all successful individual companies that Honeywell acquired because they complemented Honeywell's core business of building the world's best automation and control Systems. As a collective, they know their job is to do much more than create the thermostats for your home. These folks save lives through products that detect smoke, gas, and fire, and they are relentless in their profession.

Business Is Good and Getting Better

Tear a page from *their* book.

By now, I suspect the fire-safety group is a model for how Honeywell operates all of its subsidiaries—and they just keep getting better. If you pull a stock price chart from 2003, you'd see Honeywell (HON) drifting down to the low $20s. But then, you'd see a steady four-year climb to today's range in the low- to mid-$60s.

Who wouldn't like 300 percent return on your dough?

How did they do it?

As you know, consumers' attitudes toward safety and prevention have been forever altered post–9/11. Laws regarding commercial safety equipment have been rewritten. In response, the world is going through a major safety refit. Nearly every school, municipal building, library, airport, shopping mall, and public space now has to comply with newly stringent safety standards. So, you might think a company with a new river of cash flowing their way might take advantage of a lazy float now and then.

Not at Honeywell.

This group is vigilant about fending off complacency. Sure, they're grateful that business is good, but they also realize that there are still other players in the game. From what I saw at each company, nobody is drifting off at the competitive wheel. Quite the opposite: they are working even harder at maintaining their relevance. For example, you cannot buy Honeywell products direct from the company. They rely on a hand-selected distributor network to sell and service their products. They respect (and protect) their sales partners, and they only keep the best. At a recent Gamewell-FCI meeting, sales vice president Steve Birdsall pointed out that more than two hundred dealers were "discontinued," so the superstar distributors in the room were the select few charged with taking the products to market.

Yeah, But Do Fire Alarms Enhance the Customer "Experience"?

The short answer is YES!

Birdsall pointed out that the iPod revolutionized the music industry, and that his company intended to do the same for fire alarms.

I'd better back up a moment.

Gamewell-FCI doesn't make the alarms found in your home.

These particular units are comprehensive, high-tech installations that are site-specified by the engineering community for evacuation purposes and large-scale fire-safety workstations. They are complicated applications, to say the least. However, somebody has to be able to understand and operate these bad boys.

This is where the iPhone comparison comes in.

Birdsall said, "Sprint claims that they lost approximately 337,000 customers to the iPhone in the summer of 2007 because of Apple's user-friendly, touch-screen interface. Sprint is laboring to introduce their own new gadget phones prior to the busy Christmas season. We're doing the same thing to our business."

According to the press release, "Gamewell-FCI has developed an NGA (network graphic annunciator) that has touch-screen controls and common menu options, and is as user-friendly as your typical ATM machine." That's pretty impressive, considering this unit is capable of displaying more than five hundred text messages, executing a full building-evacuation procedure, and identifying the source of the alarm, and also contains applicable emergency contacts and locations of hazardous-material storage areas. Building managers will now have a much easier way to monitor fire systems and control the environment in case of an emergency.

Gamewell-FCI remains relevant because they don't assume that everyone knows how to fly a 747 jumbo jet. Homeowners and building managers need to be able to respond quickly and confidently in an emergency—not page through an owner's manual while buildings burn to the ground.

More companies should strive to incorporate a lower-technology user experience into their higher-tech capabilities.

"We Have a History of Looking Forward"

When I heard this slogan from Steven Rossi, vice president of communications, I thought it was brilliant. I couldn't wait to see how they backed that up claim.

I didn't wait long.

I heard president Allen Fritts tell his troops that "80 percent of today's product offerings didn't even exist three years ago." In fact, I saw several of "tomorrow's products" that weren't being shipped yet, but certainly raised the interest quotient of their salivating distributors. The distributors were excited to see new and relevant products ready to fill the future pipeline. The broad grins in the crowd telegraphed to an amateur "alarm-o-phile" like me that they were pleased to have backed the right horse. Furthermore, in the electronics industry, getting a UL approval rating is the equivalent of an FDA approval in the food business. The Honeywell Life Safety group leads the industry in getting that coveted UL ninth edition rating, the latest standard of safety for commercial fire alarm systems. Their approval is so far ahead of everyone else's that you can imagine it gives their competitors "night sweats."

Relevant Review

We all need to take technology seriously, but we can't let it be a substitute for exercising more humanity and impacting the customer's emotional experience.

Customers take technology for granted. So should you. Reliable technology is simply the price of admission today, because everyone has it. Set up technology to make life easier for your customers. Not only should your technology be user-friendly, *you* should be user-friendly.

Your greatest focus should transcend technology, aiming to understand the way human beings *interact* with technology.

Chapter 11

Your Market Research Is Probably Wrong

Dear Mr. and Mrs. Customer: What Do You Think of Us?

Researchers drive me crazy. Some do it in a good way.

You want research so you can adjust your marketing and serve your customers better, right? All organizations make themselves crazy trying to get useful feedback from their customers and clients. Sadly, they also drive customers nuts with dinner-time telemarketing, spam email blasts, annoying "free" offers in exchange for taking a survey, and exhaustive evaluation forms that read like the SATs.

Here's the raw truth: our own independent research shows that most post-transaction surveys and feedback forms actually *degrade* your customer relationship. Customers hate these surveys so much that a survey can directly cause your customers and clients to avoid future purchases from you. Stop calling them. Stop emailing them your easy-to-fill-out evaluations. Customers view these as intrusions and tests they didn't ask to take. Asking your customers and clients to articulate their experience with you is like asking them to throw darts at their own eyes.

Throw Away Your Customer/Client Evaluations

From the one thousand customer complaints we read, customers told us they were *never* in the mood to, at *your* convenience, take another test, fill out a form, or discuss their experiences.

You Aren't Getting What You Need

Most evaluation forms are worthless—not to mention exhausting, time-consuming, potentially humiliating, and arguably the single most irritating element of the buying experience.

Here's why.

First, each evaluation form is laid out differently. The form makes customers feel stupid because it takes time for them to deduce how they feel about the service they received using your measurement terms.

On a scale of one to ten, is the food a five? Is the cleanliness a seven? What if my seven is someone else's four? Will my seven cancel out someone else's three? Am I "More Likely" to come back, or am I "Least Likely" to tell other people?

Managers love written evaluations, because they think they can make decisions about people and procedures based on data. Managers also think they can design the questions to monitor how well their customer care initiatives are being executed.

But it's a flawed measurement.

Humans don't have perfect memories. Their scores are colored by their moods at that moment. Customers might be marking down high scores because you are bribing them with a discount on their next meal or offering them a prize of some kind.

On the following pages, I've reprinted a few of the evaluation forms from my book, *The Customer Shouts Back,* because this is information worth repeating.

Do you own/lease this vehicle? ☐ Yes *(Continue)* ☐ No ☐ Never owned *(If you marked 'no' or 'never owned', please return survey in envelope provided)*
Did you purchase/lease at this dealership? ☐ Yes *(Continue)* ☐ No *(Please return survey in envelope provided)*   0412241006482

Product presentation

1 Please rate your **SALESPERSON** on each of the following: ▪

	Excellent	Good	Average	Fair	Poor	Not Applicable
Prompt initial greeting	☐	☐	☐	☐	☐	
Courtesy/friendliness	☐	☐	☐	☐	☐	
Integrity	☐	☐	☐	☐	☐	
Matched vehicle to your needs	☐	☐	☐	☐	☐	
Considerate of your time	☐	☐	☐	☐	☐	
Ability to answer your questions	☐	☐	☐	☐	☐	
Test drive	☐	☐	☐	☐	☐	☐
Knowledge of models/features	☐	☐	☐	☐	☐	

Comments on question 1:

Negotiation

2 During your price/payment **NEGOTIATION** experience, how would you rate the following?

	Excellent	Good	Average	Fair	Poor
Simple and straightforward	☐	☐	☐	☐	☐
Honesty	☐	☐	☐	☐	☐
Your comfort with the process	☐	☐	☐	☐	☐
Consideration for your time	☐	☐	☐	☐	☐
Knowledge of purchase/finance options	☐	☐	☐	☐	☐

Comments on question 2:

Final paperwork

3 Thinking about the **PERSON WHO COMPLETED YOUR FINAL PAPERWORK** (financing/leasing, registration, insurance, service contracts) how would you rate the following?

	Excellent	Good	Average	Fair	Poor
Concern for your needs	☐	☐	☐	☐	☐
Courtesy/friendliness	☐	☐	☐	☐	☐
Integrity	☐	☐	☐	☐	☐
Knowledge of products/services offered	☐	☐	☐	☐	☐
Explanation of documents/paperwork	☐	☐	☐	☐	☐
Ability to answer your questions	☐	☐	☐	☐	☐
Consideration for your time	☐	☐	☐	☐	☐
Accurately completed your paperwork	☐	☐	☐	☐	☐
Fulfilled negotiated commitments	☐	☐	☐	☐	☐

Comments on question 3:

This was only the first of four pages I was asked to fill out when I bought my last car. The car dealership asked me to recall every single detail of the transaction, even the negotiation process (item two). Were the negotiations Excellent? Good? Fair? Poor? How should I know? I don't buy a car every day. I think the negotiation turned out good for *them*. So I wrote in the Comments box, "You won!"

Some of the questions were just plain dumb. "Did the vehicle match my needs?" I wrote, "Not really. I have a bad habit of spending a lot of money on unsuitable cars."

I gave up and quit writing before page two.

What's wrong with this next evaluation from a high-end hotel?

Well, the questions on the form are innocent enough. But you have to constantly twist your head sideways to read the description of your satisfaction level. The satisfaction level descriptor isn't even language you and I use every day. Have you ever described a meeting or encounter as "somewhat satisfying"? And, of course, you have to adapt to a different format than the one used in the car evaluation form.

Please rate your satisfaction with each of the following:	VERY SATISFIED	SOMEWHAT SATISFIED	NEUTRAL	SOMEWHAT DISSATISFIED	VERY DISSATISFIED
Overall satisfaction with this experience	□	□	□	□	□
Receiving a warm and sincere greeting upon arrival	□	□	□	□	□
Staff greeting you by name	□	□	□	□	□
Staff remembering you as a regular guest	□	□	□	□	□
Timeliness of check-in	□	□	□	□	□
Receiving the room you expected	□	□	□	□	□
Ability of the staff to anticipate your needs	□	□	□	□	□
Cleanliness of the guest room	□	□	□	□	□
Condition of the guest room furnishings	□	□	□	□	□
Cleanliness of the hotel	□	□	□	□	□
Condition of the hotel furnishings	□	□	□	□	□
Quality of the food	□	□	□	□	□
Receiving a fond farewell when you checked out	□	□	□	□	□

This next example is so simple that I almost liked it.

---

1. Was your room available by the check in time of 3pm?

☐YES   ☐NO

If not 3pm, around what time? _____

2. How satisfied were you with the cleanliness of your room?

☐ Exceeds Expectations   ☐ Met Expectations
☐ Did Not Meet Expectations

If we did not meet your expectations, please explain:

3. How satisfied were you with the air quality and temperature of your room?

☐ Exceeds Expectations   ☐ Met Expectations
☐ Did Not Meet Expectations

If we did not meet your expectations, please explain:

4. How satisfied were you with the knowledge of our staff you encountered during your stay? (i.e., Front Desk, Concierge...)

☐ Exceeds Expectations   ☐ Met Expectations
☐ Did Not Meet Expectations

If we did not meet your expectations, please explain:

I say "almost" because the next page of the form was very con-
fusing. They assumed I had gotten the hang of their *Exceeds, Met,
Did Not Meet Expectations* "test." Page two looks like an eye test.

	Food Quality			Quality Service			Value for Price Paid		
mark which of the following restaurants or lounges ited during your stay, and let us know how we red up.									
eeds Expectations M= Met Expectations D= Did Not Meet Expectations									
oo	E	M	D	E	M	D	E	M	D
a's	E	M	D	E	M	D	E	M	D
	E	M	D	E	M	D	E	M	D
nos	E	M	D	E	M	D	E	M	D
vers	E	M	D	E	M	D	E	M	D
h	E	M	D	E	M	D	E	M	D
en Grve	E	M	D	E	M	D	E	M	D
hin Ftn	E	M	D	E	M	D	E	M	D
na	E	M	D	E	M	D	E	M	D
sh	E	M	D	E	M	D	E	M	D
ies	E	M	D	E	M	D	E	M	D

And what makes management think that one evaluation form is
right for *every* outlet in *every* community?

One hotel manager in the southern United States told me, "I use
the forms because [the chain] tells me to, but I don't put much stock
in them. A lot of people are still pretty racist down here, so when we
get complaints, we don't know if it's related to service or skin color."

Are All Evaluations Forms Destructive?

Nope.

The Callahan Trucking Company has the most relevant and effective evaluation form I've ever seen. This company says they get 97 percent of their forms back. Customers say that the evaluation actually enhances the final moment of the transaction. This company doesn't ask a lot of you. They just want you to check the facial expression that most describes how you felt after the transaction. The back of the page is blank so you can write additional comments in your own words.

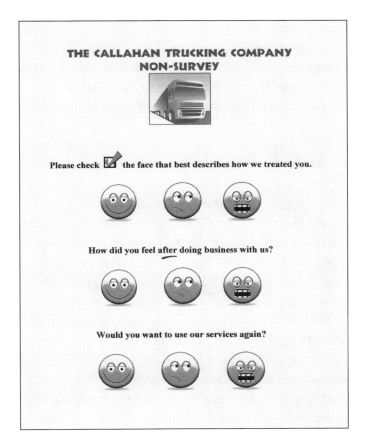

So, What's the Alternative?

If you must evaluate performance through the use of forms, at the very least take the forms away from the customer. Don't make the customer do all your work for you. Risk talking to them yourself.

"Interrogate" and Listen to Your Front Line

I know face-to-face conversation with your staff is more time-consuming than email and texting. It's also low-tech. But it's the smartest time you can spend, because the folks on the front line touch your customers every day. They hear exactly what's right and what's wrong, and will suggest ways to build your business through their frequent customer and client requests. Hold a weekly meeting for a "frontline state of the union," and be willing to realize that these people are smart and in the best position to keep you relevant.

The Staubach Company Keeps Evaluations Simple

Ross Shafer: Roger, you mentioned that you use a pretty simple customer satisfaction report, something that identifies behavior patterns without putting your clients through a forty-minute form.
Roger T. Staubach: Well, we basically have just two questions. We ask how satisfied you are with Staubach's overall performance, and how likely it is that you would recommend Staubach to a friend or colleague. And then they can actually put comments on the side, and they grade us from one to ten. If we get a nine to ten, we know that they'll promote us to their friends. Passively satisfied is seven to eight. The detractors are zero to six. We have more than five thousand transactions a year, and in most cases, we get a response back.
RS: It's easier to fill out the form when you keep it so simple.

RTS: Two questions are all we need. Let's say we're doing forty transactions for one company, and it could spread among twenty of our offices. We want to get a pattern of how we treat that particular customer, and also get an overall view of the Staubach Company in different markets. So we see all that in the simple form. We call it the Enterprise Survey Results Report, and it's a fantastic tool because it's simple to do, and if you're in the nines and tens, you're going the right direction. The seven and eight scores are good, but we've still got some work to do.

RS: Sevens and eights get your attention as a red flag?

RTS: Yes, we take a close look at that. I see the reports, and they're easy for me to read. We have the name of the client, the type of deal it was, if it was an office deal, when the survey was done, the lead office, the brokers involved, the contact name—everything. So it's pretty thorough, and it's been a phenomenal tool for us. It allows us to really "walk our talk" in order to remain customer-driven.

RS: What happens when you get a nine or ten score?

RTS: Because our people know that this report's going to come back to me, I send emails to them and compliment them when they get their tens and nines. If there are some problems, we try to understand them before we call the customer and say, "What is the issue here with this documentation? What's the problem?" I often personally get involved. It's important for our clients to understand that nothing falls through the cracks here.

This Hotel Understands You

Simple is better.

A boutique hotel chain I love installed a direct complaint phone line in every room. They put a small sign on it that says, "If you are unhappy in any way, please pick up this phone." When a customer calls, the line automatically rings the front desk. Then someone pleasantly answers, "Thank you for calling, Mr. Smith. What can we correct for you?" Then, no matter what you say, the person manning the complaint line pleasantly responds, "I apologize. I will take care of the problem" or "I will make sure management hears about this immediately." Then, *that employee* fills out the evaluation form. It's fast. It's immediate. And, it's coming directly from the customer's mouth. The other benefit is that the customer isn't stewing about this problem for the entire stay.

Beware of Focus Groups

Focus groups have too much power and too little skill.

I don't like focus groups because they are inexpert, human lab rats who cannot accurately communicate under pressure. (It's not their fault, by the way.) Besides, focus groups are the lazy way out of listening to your actual customers.

For the uninitiated, focus groups are small groups of people—say, ten to twenty-five members—who are trapped in a room, asked to watch a commercial, taste a product, or witness behaviors, and then answer questions posed by a professional question-asker called a moderator. If the focus group gives the product or service high marks, the company takes their "rating" as a reason to move ahead. But if the focus group is so prophetic, then why do eight out of ten product and service introductions fail? It's because the conditions of using the product or service are not organic. The focus group members are sequestered in an out-of-context room, participating in an experiment with other out-of-context people. The moderator can make one small reaction error and unwittingly invalidate the discussion. On top of that, there are always emerging personality dynamics. One person typically assumes the loudmouth-leader role, thereby influencing the others.

Think about it rationally. If focus groups are such a barometer of future success, it would follow that a high percentage of focus group "success stories" would create tomorrow's hit products and services—yet clearly the opposite is true.

Not to mention—people lie!

In a recent national jewelry focus group, women were asked, "Does having a large diamond make you feel good, in the sense that you can impress other women?" The women overwhelmingly answered, "No, it's more about my own personal satisfaction." But 100 percent of the jewelers we talked to laughed and said this was a total lie. One very prominent national jewelry chain owner put it this way, "Women want very much to impress other women. They want their nail person and their hairstylist to notice their diamond. They want their girlfriends to notice. It's a status symbol and of-tentimes a gesture of how much their mate loves them. But women would never admit to that much vanity."

Even knowing the fatal flaws of focus groups still does not deter some managers from gathering "test groups" for the sole reason of independently corroborating somebody's gut *emotional* feeling. Somebody in the corporate chain wants to push an idea forward but doesn't want to risk sticking out his or her own lone neck. The focus group serves as both the champion and the scapegoat. If the idea flops, the manager can always censure the focus group and say, "I don't know why the idea failed. The focus group told us they loved the product."

Let Me Drive One More Nail in the Focus Group Coffin

As a TV host and producer, I've sat in on dozens of focus-group marketing meetings to determine if a new television show should go on the air.

Here's how it works in the television business. When a TV network wants to present a new program, they shoot a test show, or pilot. Then, they test every substantial element of the pilot with potential viewers. They test the set design, the graphic elements, the music, the dialogue, and the show's premise (example: two guys share an apartment and discover they were married to the same woman). The most tested items of scrutiny are the actors and hosts. Since TV viewers are supposed to "fall in love" with the actors, the audience reaction is critical.

One day, I sat behind a focus group one-way mirror while the moderator was testing a female-host candidate. He asked the group these questions:

"Which term best describes her? Cute, pretty, or sexy?"

"Do you like her hair that way?"

"Do you like the sound of her voice? If not, please describe it."

"How about her taller height compared to the other actors?"

"Women, would you like to have her as your best friend?"

"Men, would you like to sleep with her?"

Besides the obvious offensive nature of the questions, there were several flaws in the questions asked. The questions were a result of one female executive's gut feeling "concerns," which were already biased. The focus group was asked to evaluate hair, voice and height—components that may not have occurred to them in a real world likeability test. Sometimes we are attracted to people because of their personality, laugh, or charisma, regardless of a hairstyle.

Would you like to be judged like that?

Generally, if the TV project test comes back, "positive—absolutely through the roof," then the network may order anywhere from two to thirteen episodes. If the project scores badly with test audiences, it is usually scrapped.

Here's the final and most important fatal flaw.

If you trust focus groups to be so smart, then it follows that by using their test data, *every* TV show that tested "through the roof" would become a hit series.

How wrong are they?

The latest estimates show that only 10 percent of TV pilots ever see the light of the public cathode-ray tube. Even fewer survive past the initial episode order.

Worst TV Focus Group of All Time

In 1970, the ABC network tested the TV show *All in the Family*. More than three hundred people watched the pilot and filled out survey cards. Test audiences didn't like it. So ABC backed out. CBS picked it up and did their own round of testing. The results clearly stated that Archie Bunker was too mean and uncaring. Fortunately, programming director Fred Silverman liked the show and put it on anyway. On January 12, 1971, *All in the Family* hit the airwaves as a midseason replacement and stayed in the top twenty for nine seasons.

Trust Your Gut for a Change

In my opinion, focus groups are an expensive waste of time when it comes to judging a customer's response. If you are an experienced and savvy judge of what people like, you don't need a focus group to endorse your gut.

Have some faith in your own experienced instincts.

If you believe in an idea, then have the courage of your conviction to try it. If it fails, do something else. Scientists call this experiment *failing forward*.

Instead of Focus Groups, Hire Trained Investigators

I absolutely love the mystery/secret shopper concept.

They are the best private investigators your research money can buy.

Secret shopping doesn't require any effort from the customer, and, if done correctly, it provides you with the most honest, direct feedback possible. The best feature of secret shopping is that it fills in the blanks, i.e., the feedback missing from surveys.

Judith Hess, owner of Customer Perspectives in Hooksett, New Hampshire, told me that "most [solicited] surveys are filled out by people who really like the place or really hate the place. The secret shopper represents the silent majority, the customer in the middle who never says anything and never fills out those things."

If you're not familiar with the secret-shopping process, here's a short primer. Company XYZ hires a mystery shopping company and gives their "shoppers" real money to pretend to be real shoppers. The amount of spending money per transaction can be as low as $5, depending on the price of the items being shopped. The shoppers are carefully trained to absorb everything about the shopping experience. Company XYZ has designed a report form that the shopper then fills out as a transaction "postmortem." The report may have questions like:

- Was the employee friendly?
- Was he/she attractively dressed?
- Was the employee polite? Attentive?
- How would you judge this salesperson's ability to sell?
- Did he/she attempt to cross-sell other items?
- How was this person's product knowledge?
- Did the store open (or close) on time?

Sometimes the company is pleasantly surprised. Other times, they are stunned by the bad behavior, and know exactly why sales are slipping. It's a good system—but like any system, it can be "worked."

John Saccheri owns Mystique Shopper, LLC, in Orlando, Florida. He says he has to wind his way through all kinds of flaws in the system.

"It's scary when the company who hires us wants us to create the entire report for them, or they want to use a report form that is ten or fifteen years old," Saccheri says. "We have to really work with the company to make sure the survey is relevant and that we are looking for behaviors that can help the company. Otherwise, our service has very little value."

Even phrasing the report badly can cause problems, says Saccheri.

"Companies will ask us to fill out a report where the customer service ratings are: '(1) Wow, (2) What I expected, and (3) Less than I expected.' Well, if you get a 'Wow' reaction the first time you went in, great. But you go in a second time and you know it's going to be great, so you mark down '(2) What I expected'—because the service was what I expected: great. Skews the outcome, doesn't it?

"'Yes' and 'No' are also not very helpful answers. If I go into a store and the questions is, 'Was the employee friendly?' and I answer 'No,' that isn't very helpful. Why? What did he/she do that wasn't friendly? We need a much more descriptive explanation to go with the report."

Saccheri says a lot of upper-management folks are out of touch. "We did work for a jewelry chain that built its customer base on being friendly and always offering to clean a person's jewelry. The company was famous for that service, and upper management just assumed it was always being done. After a long shopping test, we found out that in all of the visits, only one customer was offered a free jewelry cleaning. Management couldn't believe it. They took the process for granted."

And, the employees learn how to work the system, too. They know they are eventually going to be "shopped," so they watch for telltale signs. They watch for patterns, Saccheri says.

"Management will often ask for a planned sequence of events to happen. They will tell us to first send our people to the bar for a drink, then sit down for dinner, and finally visit the dance club or whatever. Well, employees are smart. They look for patterns. If they catch on to the pattern, they will eliminate customers who don't follow the sequence. It's not a perfect system—pretty close, but not perfect."

Hess told me that employees are very defensive and use lots of excuses for not being polite—or for not repeating the customer's name.

"They will say something like, 'I didn't say their name because it was a foreign name and I didn't want to insult them by mispronouncing it,' or, 'I didn't know if I should say "Mrs.," "Ms.," or "Miss," so I didn't say anything.' But these are all excuses, and none of them are acceptable."

Some employees fight "the report."

When there is a large bonus attached to an employee's customer-service behavior, you can bet that employees will fight even harder for their right to blame the customer. Saccheri told me about a car dealership that had a very strict customer-service policy. The procedure required employees to (1) offer customers a test drive, (2) offer to appraise their used cars, (3) offer to explain all the features of the new car, and about five other "must-do" items. When one employee was presented with the shopper report, he vehemently contested it. He got angry and convinced the sales manager that he had, in fact, offered the customer every one of those "must-do" items. There was a big bonus riding on the review, and he didn't think he was being treated fairly. In fact, he demanded to be "re-shopped."

Saccheri explained: "Unfortunately, the next time the salesman was *video*-shopped. When he was shown, on the tape, that he had forgotten to do several things that he was supposed to do, he still asked for a reprieve, citing a number of unrelated excuses. And the sales manager let it go."

Both Hess and Saccheri told me that good customer service teeters on the shaky shoulders of management, and that many of them just don't "buy into" the program. They don't see customer relations as financially important as it is.

"They are all about getting the operations right," Hess says. "Everybody has so much to do and is so busy—and there are so many layers in these big organizations—that even if the CEO says he wants a stronger customer-service push, it gets lost by the time it reaches the bottom management rung."

Saccheri agrees. "Many of these managers say they want to improve customer service, but when they get the results, they are in denial about it because it reflects on them."

Both Saccheri and Hess told me that the best shift they have seen in their business is that more companies are using shoppers to "catch people doing things right." Companies want the mystery shopper *not* to be viewed as a policeman, but rather as a positive part of creating a good customer-service culture. When discourteous employees see others being rewarded for good behavior, it makes a strong enough (financial) impression to get them to try being nice.

If you think about it, secret shopping was the first "reality" TV show.

Ethnography Rules!

People lie.

Reality TV has taught us that we will tune into a program featuring nonprofessional actors because their reactions are authentic. We are eavesdropping on people just like us as they live and react in their natural habitats.

That's why ethnography has become so effective in determining behaviors. Regardless of what your customers, clients, or patients *say* they do, observing people as they experience different sources of stress and circumstances reveals *what they really do.*

Ethnography is the study of watching human behavior and lightly participating in it—hopefully without interfering or influencing that behavior. The cool thing about watching behavior is that it's real.

The research subject isn't lying over the phone or deceiving you on a survey sheet. In fact, ethnography is fast becoming the preferred way to accurately track true customer behaviors. Dr. Norman Stolzoff, founder of Ethnographic Insight, is a cultural anthropologist who acts as a hired gun for companies such as Banana Republic, JCPenney, 3M, InfoSpace, and Expedia to create detailed ethnographic studies of their customers. His job is to spend months analyzing and documenting human behaviors as they relate to commerce. Though his research is proprietary and not available for publication here, I believe in the approach and have used it in my case studies.

Drug Companies Need to Know This

"Does our drug really work?"

Companies like GlaxoSmithKline (GSK) produce ethnographic films to understand the psychology of people who have either success or failure with the medicinal drugs they take. I saw a short film that casually observed the behaviors of patients with Type 2 diabetes, and how their behavior related to the efficacy of their medications. GSK wanted to know, "Did the meds we prescribed work for you?" I watched patients say that they take the pills—and watched family members catch them in the lie. What makes people lie about something proven to make them healthier? Embarrassment is one reason. Secondly, taking medication is an admission that something is wrong. People don't like to admit that they are sick enough to need these drugs for a lifetime. That can sound like a death sentence to some patients.

The films also revealed that success and failure often may be related to the health-care professional's attitude. Among cases in which the doctors wrote prescriptions after cursory examinations, the patients tended to take the meds haphazardly, if at all. Among cases in which the doctors wrote prescriptions after taking time to get to know the patients, then made frequent follow-up phone calls to monitor progress, the patients experienced marked success. Watching authentic behavior in the use of GSK products gave GSK the insight they needed to address the doctor-patient "teaching" relationship.

JCPenney Used Ethnography to Help Come Back from the Grave

JCPenney nearly went extinct.

Many wonder how JCPenney, an American icon, stumbled into a downward spiral. The answer is that they became irrelevant. Macy's grew in stature and posed a national threat. Target and Wal-Mart became more significant in the clothing equation. And smaller competitors, such as Abercrombie and Fitch, Diesel, Ralph Lauren—even microbrands such as Sean Jean—became more fashionable and appealing to consumers. JCPenney became the place your dad bought his annual supply of underwear.

Yet just five years ago, JCPenney resurfaced as a retail powerhouse. A company with a 2001 stock price hovering around $10 has steadily increased that price to over $80 per share as of this writing. How did they pull that off? One important factor, in my opinion, was that JCPenney added a full-time employee with a PhD in cultural anthropology who studies the actual behaviors of their customers and their competitors. When they applied this research to their online bridal registry, it virtually revolutionized how brides shop for gifts.

Only a handful of the companies I've seen have taken this bold step.

Instead of sending out surveys or imposing on customers during the dinner hour with annoying phone calls, relevant organizations revel in trying to understand how humanity operates and behaves naturally. By observing buyers in their natural state, their habits will be obvious—and not tainted by how organizations think they *should* be answering the questions.

Relevant Review

We often make the customer work too hard trying to articulate and evaluate their experience with us. It's not their job to review our work. They aren't thinking about it along the way; consequently, the only part of the experience they are likely to remember is the final moment.

If you use evaluation forms, rethink how they are structured and the questions you ask. Don't make people judge you with words or descriptors they don't use in their day-to-day lives.

Scrap focus groups. They are a waste of time and won't give you useful information or answers.

Instead, try using ethnography to determine how your customers, clients, and patients *really* behave when they use your products and services. Ethnography doesn't lie.

Hire professionals to *secret shop* your business. These trained professionals will report the worst—and, hopefully, the best—you have to offer. Their information is unbiased and accurate, and offers an opportunity to catch people doing things right! That's incredibly inspiring and useful information!

Chapter 12

Go Green or Go Home

When Jeff Immelt, CEO of General Electric, uttered the phrase "Green is green," there was a collective corporate gasp heard around the world. It was the first time a major-league executive admitted that being environmentally friendly had profitable implications. It was as if the dirty little secret had finally been unearthed.

Social Responsibility Is Better for Your Stakeholders

Care about other people, and they will care for you.

When people understand that buying from your company also means a positive contribution to their favorite causes—whether it's the environment, pet rescue, cancer research, or other important issues—they feel a shared sense of values with you. Maybe they don't directly make charitable donations throughout the course of the year, but they can feel good if they know that they are supporting a company that is doing good works—or even better, if part of the money they spend with you is directly donated to a particular cause. We all do it—even if it's subconscious. Every day, you and I pay more money to feel better—physically and emotionally—because of the internal and external stresses we endure. Consider the multiple crises our world has experienced in the last seven years. Most of our recent catastrophes were totally out of our control.

The stock market melted down in 2000. The terrorist attacks of September 11, 2001, created a culture of fear that has not left us. We went to war with Iraq in 2003. Major corporate scandals—such as those perpetrated by Enron, WorldCom, HealthSouth, and Arthur Andersen—left their employees' retirement plans bone-dry. When employees are refused a raise in pay, but read about grossly inflated CEO salaries, it furthers a feeling of corporate mistrust and anger. The global economy may be good for business, but many Americans see the off-shoring of labor as stealing food from the mouths of their children. And now, in the midst of this lingering war in Iraq, more and more Americans are feeling frustrated and helpless. Americans loathe feeling helpless. They want to take action, and they want *you* to take action *for* them.

I Want to Do My Part

Most of our lives are out of our control.

While we can't stop wars or eliminate corporate thievery, changing the environment is something we concerned citizens think we can do something about. But we know we can't do it alone. Sure, we can all recycle our bottles and cans. We can install water-saving devices in our toilets. Some of us can even afford to buy hybrid cars. But most consumers feel those are small steps compared to what a large corporation might be able to do. They think, "Why don't they put their financial resources to work and fix this thing?" The good news is that these consumers' wallets and purses stand ready to support you if you participate in the green movement.

According to corporate environmental expert Tim Sexton:

> A brand that understands it has a relationship with its customers and audience, per se, knows the value of having shared values with that audience and a concern for their greater good. Consumers are smart and aware of the environment and our dependence on fossil fuels from the Middle East—so not only do they recycle and give money to green causes, they don't want to contribute to a company who haphazardly goes about destroying the planet. Being truly conscious of doing business in a responsible way really matters to people. Customers want to feel good about the way you do business because they feel (in an ancillary way) that they are contributing to the health of the environment in a passive way.

Sexton runs The Sexton Company. His company not only produced the "Live Aid" and "Live 8" mega rock concerts, it also specializes in teaching good-citizen behaviors to corporations and institutions through innovative strategies and tactical plans. Sexton shows them how they can "do well by doing good." One of their clients is the Philadelphia Eagles NFL football team.

Football's Eagles Go Green

After nearly a decade of rehabilitating his NFL franchise, Philadelphia Eagles owner Jeffrey Lurie wanted to find a way to forge a connection between the team and its fans that was unrelated to the team's performance. Lurie understood that the loyalty of Eagles fans—and of the citizens of Philadelphia in general—would be strengthened if the organization, as Sexton suggested, shared values with its citizens and showed a concern for the greater good. It would be this deeper connection that Lurie hoped would sustain support for the team, even when the on-field performance was not at its best. With the help of The Sexton Company, the "Go Green" program was born.

The team wanted to rally the community to join them in increasing environmental responsibility, particularly in the Philadelphia area. Lincoln Financial Field, the home of the Eagles since 2003, is devoted to recycling and waste reduction at all stadium events, and the Eagles organization itself is the leading recycler in the city. They also are one of the leading purchasers of renewable energy in the coal-dependent state of Pennsylvania. This statistic is particularly significant, given that Pennsylvania contributes a staggering 1 percent of the planet's greenhouse gases.

As word of the Eagles' commitment to being a market leader in going "green" has spread, increased goodwill in the city and state has spread as well. The organization stands as an example of genuine global concern and a commitment to positive action.

Erin Brockovich Couldn't Catch Them Now

Wow, nothing like having your mistakes made into a movie!

In 1996, Pacific Gas and Electric (PG&E) was a company in need of some image rehab. They had just lost a $333 million lawsuit against the residents of Hinkley, California. PG&E was convicted of contaminating their drinking water with toxic hexavalent chromium. The public-relations pain was elevated to a global level when the case was dramatized on the big screen in the 2000 film, *Erin Brockovich,* starring Julia Roberts.

But more than ten years later, with a new and socially energized CEO at the helm, the company's efforts to reduce global warming are clearly focused on doing right.

Late in 2006, CEO Peter A. Darbee convened a group of the world's leading scientists on climate change, including Bob Coral, Amory Lovins, and Joel Swisher. The seminar left PG&E management convinced that global warming is real, humanity is contributing to the phenomena, and we must act now to stem the tide. Darbee also was made aware that public utility companies account for 40 percent of all production of greenhouse gases. So he and his team immediately dove into the challenge.

PG&E is exploring technologies such as plug-in hybrid vehicles that would be able to charge their batteries at night, when electricity is cheaper, and then sell the electricity back into the grid during the daytime. The company also is looking at the possibility of harvesting wind in Canada and transmitting the energy it is capable of producing back to California, thus creating a more environmentally friendly energy source for its customers. The company also is actively involved in helping to develop tidal-generation technologies that take advantage of ocean currents to produce electricity.

Furthermore, PG&E placed advertisements all over San Francisco (perhaps most noticeably on the scoreboard and backstop at AT&T Park during Barry Bond's highly televised pursuit of the Major League Baseball all-time homerun record in the summer of 2007) that read, "Let's Green This City." Not only were they making genuine efforts, they wanted people to notice their commitment to environmentalism, and they wanted to send the message that San Francisco should lead the way in the cause. Smart works, indeed. But invariably PG&E's marketing department would ask, "Yeah, but does anybody notice what we do?"

Thus far, the answer has been yes. As the company has developed a reputation for environmental leadership, it has seen its customer-approval ratings soar and its California Public Utilities Commission (CPUC) and political standing improve significantly. Darbee has been asked to testify several times before U.S. Senate committees on environmental concerns about greenhouse gases.

Small Green Efforts Matter

Many corporate meetings are reducing their carbon footprint by cutting back or eliminating the use of bottled water (less plastic), providing only one glass of water at meals instead of two (less washing of glassware), offering no red meat on the menu (to reduce methane gas production—yes, somebody has researched this), circulating fewer paper handouts (to reduce wasted paper products), and printing programs with soy ink on recycled paper.

If You Go Green, You'd Better Mean It.

Once your company has made the decision to become a good-citizen brand, it is crucial that you follow these words of advice: don't fake it—be authentic. An unfortunate consequence of the demand and desire for businesses to become socially responsible and environmentally friendly has been the advent of "greenwashing" and "bluewashing." Companies that greenwash are environmental polluters that publicly advertise themselves as "green" or environmentally friendly. Similarly, bluewashing (a reference to the color blue in the United Nations logo) is a phenomenon in which companies publicly advertise good, socially responsible activities—such as fair trade and labor practices—while doing the opposite in actual practice. In this age of technology and free flow of information, it is virtually impossible for businesses to hide their true colors. Don't try to fool your customers. If you are dishonest, they will discover the truth. To be publicly labeled a greenwasher or bluewasher could be financially crippling. Oftentimes, the most blatant greenwashers and bluewashers are those companies that go to great lengths to shout out to the world how wonderful they are. When Shakespeare wrote, "The lady doth protest too much, methinks," he could have been anticipating such organizations.

So, how do you go about increasing public and consumer goodwill toward your brand without appearing to toot your own horn? Again, the key here is to be authentic. *Genuine* good works never stay a secret. Word of mouth and third-party endorsements are always the fastest paths to increasing goodwill. News outlets are always looking for the next feel-good story, and an article or story that ends up doing the touting for you has a much more genuine and authentic feel to it.

Need More Convincing
That Social Consciousness Is Relevant?

Social consciousness has become a college course.

Currently, more than half the business schools in the United States offer courses on corporate social responsibility and/or environmental stewardship. However, while current business students will eventually enter the workplace armed and ready to face these issues, those already in the business world need to adjust to this ever-growing trend.

What social issues turn your stomach the most? Go with your gut. How your organization chooses to address this is up to you. Nothing is more fundamentally authentic than a cause about which you are genuinely passionate.

Being socially conscious is not only a good strategy for differentiating yourself from your competitors, it is actually a way to become your industry leader. Be the first in your industry to convert to renewable energy sources, attack local and global poverty, or rehabilitate schools or neighborhoods. When a customer or client is choosing among brands, it just may be your good deeds that sway their decision toward your brand.

Relevant Review

It is not my place to debate the pros and cons of greenhouse gases or the causes of global warming. All I can do is report how companies are reacting to the publicity storm from these environmental phenomena.

Your customers, clients, and patients have shown a great interest in this topic, and so should you. They are more prone to give money to companies who are "issue conscious" over companies who don't take such a stand; so, it makes sense economically to be aware of the carbon footprints you leave behind. Simply stated: if you care about our planet and the people on it, your customers will feel better about giving you their money.

Find an issue that makes your heart race, and get behind it. Then ask your customers to join you in the fight. Taking a stand helps galvanize your company's attitude, point of view, and brand. It's the right thing to do. Are you afraid you might "back the wrong horse"? Stop worrying about that. Who can find fault with you if your mission is to do good?

Chapter 13

Don't Let Your Expertise Expire

The purpose of this book has been about keeping your eyes and ears open to new ideas so you can survive and thrive in any economy. We should all adopt a policy of continuous learning. We should all pay attention to great ideas—even those outside of your industry—and adapt them to yourself and your organization.

Attend the Wrong Convention

Crash a hotel near you.

Yes, I'm actually asking you to sneak your way into a big general meeting at a hotel near you. Find out what big convention is in town. Dress well, show up, and tell security at the door that you don't have your badge but that you can't miss the guest speaker;

none of these are lies, by the way. Probably 95 percent of the time you will be able to sit down and soak up some information that has the potential to revolutionize your business.

In my line of work, I get the opportunity to attend eighty-plus conferences and conventions each year. I have a front-row seat to a myriad of best practices, and then I get to do my best to cross-pollinate them at the next conference.

For example, at a large grocery chain conference, I heard an executive from Pillsbury say, "At 4:00 PM, 42 percent of grocery customers have no idea what they will be having for dinner that night."

The next week I spoke to a two hundred–unit restaurant chain. I proposed that they try adjusting their radio advertising campaign to start at 3:00 PM—because that's the time people will start thinking about dinner. They took the advice, and now their restaurant sales are up because those same confused grocery shoppers now have an idea of what they can do for dinner.

How to Keep a Family Business Relevant

Are you in business with your dad?

I honor any family who works hard to build up a family business, and then has offspring who want to take over the reins when the previous generation wants to retire. However, there is a tendency for some family businesses to insist that the next generation of management try to behave like the older generation.

That's why I applaud people like Ira Bryck, who created the Family Business Center at the University of Massachusetts. Bryck is a product of a family business himself, and he knows the pitfalls of transferring ownership and management styles within the family. His approach to challenge family members and keep them thinking in relevant terms is remarkable—and may be necessary for some of these venerable businesses to survive.

Ross Shafer: You believe that you have been able to challenge family businesses in Massachusetts to stay relevant. How do you approach this?

Ira Bryck: I swear that I invented the phrase "learning community," but since everybody else is using it, I probably just picked it up somewhere. Basically, what I think I've created is a community of people who describe themselves as nonjoiners and cynics of fads and management theories. I also know my audience. As successful as they are, they don't think of themselves as great thinkers. So to keep their interests piqued and get them talking with one another, we bring in challenging speakers to shake them up. That's why we had you come in.

The other thing about closely held businesses is that they're run by very secretive people. I think that's part of the reason why they hire family members. It's like a phrase in the Mafia called "omertà," which translates to, "If you tell, you die." Family businesses keep things very close to the vest. I came from retail, where I sold underpants, Boy Scout uniforms, Girl Scout uniforms, suits and dresses, etc. We sold thousands of items. Here, I sell wisdom, in the form of outside speakers, experience, frankness, and honesty. And that's where I feel like I need to stay ahead of other organizations, like a chamber of commerce, or a Rotary, or a trade association. When they get together at one of those meetings, they do a lot of chest pounding, or do a lot of bragging. They really can't get down in the dirt of that honest discussion like we do. I've been told many times by my members that they feel more wise and honest and frank in my room than even in other organizations.

RS: How is your organization different?

IB: I really have made it a point that you can ask a stupid question and you can disagree with the speaker, and on evaluations, many times the gem I get is something that another audience member said while disagreeing with the presenter. And so I really do try to make this a learning community in which the learning is a two-way street.

RS: You also believe the diversity of your group works in its favor.

IB: I do. A lot of people tell me that they belong to trade associations. And what I say to them is, "OK, so you get together with a thousand other precision machinists. You all have the same problems and you all have the same solutions, and I'm a believer that you can't think out of the box in that setting. You can only *really* think with people who are *not* in your box, so you need to get together with a diverse population, and build that diverse population." We've figured out a way that people can talk about what they have in common, which is nothing obvious.

RS: You would get along well with the business trainer Joel Barker. He is a huge fan of cross-pollination of diverse ideas.

IB: I know about Joel Barker. But what he says is that you always run out of the useful thoughts and you always need a wacky outsider. The wacky outsider is always the person that's going to say, "Why don't you have the customer surrogate?" I think that I have given permission to people to take a risk in the room. The other thing I repeat so often is the scene in the movie *Annie Hall*, where Woody Allen and Diane Keaton are walking down the street, and Woody Allen stops her and says, "Gimme a kiss ... because we're just gonna go home later, right? ... And there's gonna be all that tension. You know, we never kissed before, and I'll never know when to make the right move or anything. So we'll kiss now, we'll get it over with, and then we'll go eat. OK? ... And we'll digest our food better." So I frequently will say to my audience, "I give you permission to kiss. I give you permission to be brave, to talk about things that you're nervous talking about."

RS: What would they be nervous talking about?

IB: A lot of them feel ashamed. They'll say, "We are the most dysfunctional family." And then I say, "Raise your hand if you were raised in a dysfunctional family." Everybody raises their hand. I say, "OK. Get over it."

RS: You are providing safety in a high-level university setting.

IB: Right. And it's normalized. People go home from the first meeting, and a lot of times they'll say, "I don't know what I learned specifically, but I feel so much more normal." And one of the biggest learning disabilities is thinking that you have a learning disability. So if I say, "I want you to be able to go home with one thing you're going to do differently," that's not a huge task. They can do it.

RS: The "no-stupid-questions-and-no-stupid-answers" rule?

IB: Right. My father had an expression in Yiddish that, when translated, said, "From a fool, you can also learn." What I say is, "From a retailer, you can also learn. From a hospitality person, you can also learn. Just stay open to the fact that somebody tonight is going to say something that's going to save you time, money, aggravation, and so on."

RS: You meet once a month. How do you select your topic?

IB: I always try to keep my ear to the ground to hear where people are suffering. They have frank conversations with people. I'm always doing these mini focus-group conversations with whoever I get on the phone. I ask, "How are you doing?" "Where does it hurt?" "What does the quarter look like for you?" If I start to see themes, then I'll say, "OK, we're going to do a program on 'blank'."

I feel like a bumblebee. If I pick up this piece of pollen from over here, I may drop it over there. I'm saying, "Does this pollen from retail help you over here in manufacturing?" And then if a lot of people tell me, "You know what's frustrating to me is I hear all these great theories, and I never know how to plug them in, and my siblings and my parents and my cousins back at work create a real problem for me," and I'll start to say, "You know what, here is a disease that's very common." This person thinks that they're the only one to suffer like that, but it's very common.

So then I'll start to gather info for my next meeting. I have a long list of speakers and topics and I might think of three or four people who I think can tell great relevant stories about "Here's how we deal with resistance from family members." "Here's how we realize that we're about to hit an iceberg." "Here's how we figure out our options." "Here's how we figured out that it was worth the time and money to fix things in this way." Invariably someone will leave the meeting saying, "You know, I think we just figured out how to drop being a manufacturing company and become a marketing company."

Join the Wrong Trade Association

Pay dues to a club you normally wouldn't.

That's right. I'm encouraging you to join a trade organization in an industry which, on the surface, has nothing to do with what you do. If you become an associate member of a trade association—one that is wildly different from your own—and then attend their annual meetings, you will be exposed to fresh, new ideas and innovations that your own industry group may not have on their radar. If you are an engineer, join the Hospital Administration Society. If you are a nurse, join the American Trucking Association. Listen to their hired speakers. Go to their exhibit halls. Make friends and tell them why you are there. Since you are from an outside industry, they won't perceive you as competition. They will share anything and everything with you. These meetings can be fertile ground for new ideas your industry hasn't thought of—or even been exposed to yet.

Wait, Ross: Are You Saying Nurses
Can Cross-Pollinate Ideas from Truckers?

Yes. It is life-changing to know how one segment of our economic culture is affected by another.

To give you an idea of how radically our culture is shifting, look at the trucking industry. The trucking industry is going through a major cultural shift in that they are scrambling to find new drivers. Nobody wants to drive large tractor-trailers cross-country anymore. Drivers want shorter routes so that they can sleep in their own beds every night. That emotional and behavioral shift has flipped the trucking industry on its head. Since many of the new drivers are younger Millennials born after 1980, they honor the same work-life balance as their Millennial executive counterparts. You can't entice these drivers with more money, because that's not as important to them as being home with their families.

How has the trucking industry adjusted? They try to recruit husband-and-wife teams who don't mind sharing their lives on the long hauls. Trucking companies are buying smaller trucks and rerouting shipping to regional centers, so a driver can complete his route and be home for dinner.

OK, back to the nursing connection. If you are a nurse in Nebraska who has noticed less serious injuries from long haul-driver accidents, you now know why. You would also be right to assume that health-care costs will adjust to reflect inner city accident rates, regional shorter haul trucking, and so on.

Everybody affects everybody.

Read Magazines You Don't Read

Do you buy the same old magazines?

Then from now on, go to your local newsstand (or go online) and read a variety of publications you normally wouldn't read—and not just trade magazines. Pick strange magazines about science, medicine, sports, money, guitars, women's issues, or whatever. Get a sense of what our culture is talking about. Find out how people are spending their leisure time. How are they spending their money? Listen to people talk at the supermarket, the drugstore, the fast-food restaurant, the hardware

store—wherever. Remember the stock-market craze of the late
'90s? Clerks at Baskin and Robbins were volunteering "stock
tips" with a Rocky Road cone.

By researching the culture, you are listening for "buzz." Buzz is
the new stuff everybody is talking about.

You want to be the buzz.

Young people know about buzz. They are often the earliest
adopters of technology, games, phone services, and anything else
fun and interesting.

Interrogate Your Millennials

One of the hidden gold mines in your quest to remain relevant
lies in the habits and behaviors of your younger workers. They are
probably light-years ahead of you in terms of tech, fashion, trends,
and the most popular current web phenomenon. Ask them to brief
you on pop culture. Ask them who is popular and why. Ask them to
suggest a CD you should buy or a website you should visit. Then pay
attention to their suggestions, and ask more questions.

Stalk Relevant People

Once you spot a trend, go where those relevant people congregate
and talk to them. Participate in forums and blogs. Tell the bloggers
what you do, and ask them what they know about the trend. Visit
or create a MySpace page. Create a Facebook site. Frequent www.
Wikipedia.org. Better yet, create a Wikipedia page for your organization, then invite your customers and clients to visit the site and
add to it if they like. Go to www.YouTube.com and type in things
you want to know about. Find a subject you love, and join the bloggers there. It's free, and you can jump into the game anytime.

By the way, just because these particular culture-shakers are relevant today, don't think you've mastered the game. Watching for the next wave is an ongoing process.

Are Blogs Still Relevant?

Because of the viral nature of fads, many people wonder if cultural explosions like blogging have already passed them by. Don't forget, blogging—also considered social media—has only been around for about ten years. It was barely a blip on the radar screen not long ago. And blogging wasn't costly. Ease of entry was something that was simple to do. Before long, it started to explode exponentially. Still, a lot of companies ignored the blogging craze. They didn't think it was relevant until it reached that critical mass. By then, many key players had already established their positions in the blogging world. Today, companies shouldn't be on the leading edge. They *need* to be on the cutting edge.

The problem with a lot of blogs is that the content isn't fresh. You've got to post a blog at least three times a week. Adding fresh content to your site keeps people coming back. Roger Staubach of The Staubach Company posts a new blog almost every day. Mark Cuban, owner of the Dallas Mavericks, sometimes posts several times a day. If you set up a blog and only post new content four times a year, your customers will judge you as irrelevant and "old school."

Blog Your Way to the Top

Everyone who has a website wants it to show up on the first search page. I found a little trick that might help you. Google has what's called a Freshbot. It's an algorithm that has Google "spiders" scan the Internet looking for fresh content on blogs and websites. People who post new things with regularity get much better search-engine rankings.

The Next Big Thing?

For those of you who already are taking advantage of MySpace, Facebook, Wikipedia, podcasts, and YouTube, you probably want to know what the next big tech thing will be. Many experts are saying the video blog is the best candidate. Some of you may know that crude video blogs already exist on YouTube and eBaum's World. Check out "Lonely Girl," "Lisa Nova," or "Les Loken," and you'll see that some of their video blogs have a viewership of over one million. But for a business, there is technology available that will allow you to put together your own virtual news station or home-based broadcast. The software is out there, and it's cheap. Naturally, the software changes constantly, so you will need to do a search and watch the state-of-the-art evolution.

Think Like a Broadcaster

It's important to keep the quality of your video blog high and the talent side as professional as possible, because you will be judged against people who know a lot about broadcasting. Since the "air time" is free, video blogging can be a stunningly effective marketing tool for small businesses.

Video Email Rocks ... at Least for Now

Video email is sent like regular email, but you have the option of embedding a Flash video clip of you or someone from your team talking. It's cheap, and it could quickly separate you from your competition.

What I like about video email is that it bridges the widening gap between technology and humanity, with the emphasis on humanity. People need to talk to one another again—voice to voice and face to face. Some of the call centers I've worked with are experimenting with Apple's iChat. Apple computers now come with a video camera and microphone as standard equipment. With cameras and microphones on both ends, customers love the accountability of the "human" experience. With a broadband connection, the image latency (that jittery slow motion look) is gone. And, when the customer can see and hear the support person, they feel like someone is actually listening to their issues.

There are several video email companies ready and waiting for your money, but you'll have to be patient as you experiment with the technology. I first tried video email through a multi-level marketing company called TalkFusion. Their software will let you customize a video template to promote your brand, your website, or whatever. But while the technology looks cool, I could not get it to work consistently with our Windows XP computers. (Yes, you can blame me for not being in the Vista world yet).

On the other hand, I've had great success with a company called SightSpeed (www.sightspeed.com). I found their program to be extremely user-friendly and fast to upload. It not only offered video email, but several teleconferencing options as well. Here's the bonus: at this time, thirty-second video emails are free! If you want longer video emails, it will only cost you about $4.95/month.

If you need a customized business template, take a look at www. Unikron.com. The templates allow you to upload your personal-logo banner and contact information. It's a little more expensive, but worth it. The video and audio reproductions are dead on. Also check out ImageMind and HelloWorld to see which system might work best for you.

Whatever you do, stop sending boring text messages and text emails. Get visual.

Never Stop Innovating!

Never stop rethinking.

Innovation will be more important than ever when you consider that the top ten jobs in 2020 have not even been invented yet.

As I've discussed, the Honeywell Life Safety Division has a product line in which 60 percent of their products didn't even exist three years ago.

Companies like 3M are never satisfied with exceeding sales goals on today's great products. They take enormous pride in the fact that 30 percent of their products didn't even exist four years ago. They innovate to remain relevant.

Appoint a CRO (Chief Relevance Officer)

I'm not asking you to add a new person to your payroll. But somebody on your staff is probably naturally curious. Curious people ask a lot of questions and are fascinated by new information.

Note: If you don't have a single curious person in your organization, sell this book on eBay immediately. I can't help you.

Just like banking institutions that, after the Patriot Act and the Sarbanes-Oxley Act, assigned someone from the current staff to be the "compliance officer," you can periodically appoint a different coworker to become the CRO. This person is responsible for uncovering anything new, cool, and innovative inside or outside your industry. At your staff meetings, this person reports the findings and asks for any other ideas that might be new or fun. Then, make sure you publish the reports in your e-newsletter or blog so that everyone gets the information.

Relevant Review

You are running an enterprise that is supposed to be filling a specific need or want for your customers, clients, and patients. If you are a public company, you have stockholders who trust you with their hard-earned savings. For those reasons, you owe it to all these people to stay in business. You owe it to them to keep abreast of the culture shifts and technological advances that may affect them. You owe it to them to continue to improve your operations and keep prices within their reach. If you don't, your competition will find a way to eat you alive.

Staying relevant means learning everything you can about people, human nature, human behavior, medicine, sports, finance, international relations, and the future.

The survival of your company—and your career—depends on it.

Chapter 14

Learn from Two Highly Relevant Superstars

At the beginning of this book, I said that many of these organizations do a lot of things to remain relevant. But few actually nail *everything* they need to do to stay relevant.

Well, I've found two companies that *everyone* can envy, both in sheer growth and in relevant culture. You'll really enjoy reading about Zappos and BDA.

Superstar Number One: Zappos Explodes!

I won't lie to you. Writing a book is tedious work.

Nearly every page requires a ton of research, fact checking, and countless hours of rewriting. As rewarding as it is to unearth great stories, only a few are so exciting that

you can't wait to sit down and write about them. It's inspiring and exhilarating. It's exactly like a great campfire tale you've heard and can't wait to retell to your friends.

Zappos.com is such a story.

My sister-in-law, Nicole Dale, is the COO of Harveys Industries—most famous for their "Seatbelt Bag" handbags made from automobile seat-belt material. Dale also is the co-owner of an upscale fashion boutique in Santa Ana, California, called "Hannah Bean." Needless to say, Dale is "plugged in" to the fashion world. When she heard about this book, she asked me if I knew about Zappos.com, an online retailer based in Las Vegas. I hadn't. Maybe you haven't, either. But you will never forget them after you read their incredible true story of growth and relevance.

Zappos began life in 1999 with an idea to become the Amazon.com of online shoe sales. They rightfully figured if people were willing to buy books and airline tickets online, buying apparel over the Internet couldn't be far behind. That first year they humbly describe their volume as "almost nothing." But check out their staggering sales numbers beyond their first year:

1999: almost nothing
2000: $1.6 million
2001: $8.6 million
2002: $32 million
2003: $70 million
2004: $184 million
2005: $370 million
2006: $597 million
2007: $840 million

They are projecting sales of more than $1 billion for 2008! And these aren't fantasy numbers by any stretch. Their research has determined that by 2010, total U.S. footwear sales will exceed $50 billion a year. Online footwear sales will account for 10 percent of that—that's $5 billion a year. Since Zappos is the clear leader in this area, they are convinced that if they continue to focus on and improve the customer experience, they should account for 20 percent of all online footwear sales.

Their confidence is backed up by logic and competence.

How Did They Come So Far So Fast?

Zappos' growth is not just about having great software to execute the online purchase transaction. They recognized (and addressed) the emotional triggers that were pulled when customers buy products online. Back in 1999, buying any merchandise over the Internet was a risky proposition for most people. People who communicated via email or instant messaging (IM) trusted those "transactions" because they didn't have to give out personal financial information. But splashing their credit-card information over the 'net was quite another issue. Besides the threat of identity theft, what if they bought something online and didn't like it. Would they have any luck getting a refund?

Zappos understood the customer's point of view, and they eliminated all the risk. If you buy shoes from them and don't like them, they will refund you 100 percent of the purchase price—and they also will pay for the return shipping! The customer experience is so important to Zappos that they require every new hire in their Las Vegas headquarters to go through a four-week "customer loyalty" program. Three weeks are spent in Las Vegas answering phone calls from customers, and one week is spent in their Kentucky distribution center. It's extremely expensive to do this, but since they want the Zappos brand to be associated with top-tier customer service, even accountants, lawyers, and software developers go through this same training process.

Loyal Customers Matter at Zappos

Zappos has done such an incredible job of attracting and cod-dling their customers that the next challenge would obviously be to retain them. No worries there. According to Zappos own web site, they claim to have more than 7.4 million paying customers, representing approximately 2.5 percent of the U.S. population. Or to put it another way: approximately one out of every forty people in the United States is a Zappos customer.

They keep customers engaged by inviting them to participate on the company blog (http://blogs.zappos.com). As CEO Tony Hsieh describes it, "(the blog) is meant to be 'fun and a little weird'—one of our core values at Zappos."

He goes on to explain that culture and brand are one and the same, as far as he is concerned. "We will continue to build our brand and our culture because in the long run, brand and culture are the same thing. Every great, enduring company has a strong culture, and we hope one day to be one of those companies."

Back in 2003, Hsieh wrote on the company blog: "Although we happen to sell shoes today, we've built and will continue to build the platform for a great customer experience. This will allow us to one day expand into other categories beyond just shoes. But for now, it's important for us to remain focused on being the leader in online footwear sales, in terms of both selection and service."

What is significant about this business model (and the leadership behind it) is that while Zappos is obviously a company devoted to state-of-the-art software development and execution in the online world, the constant watchword comes back to human-ity. Customer service and the customer experience are the root rea-sons for their explosive growth.

Going Beyond Footwear

Hsieh followed through on his vision, and today Zappos.com has expanded into other lucrative categories, including:
- Apparel
- Sunglasses
- Watches
- Bags
- Bedding/linens
- Cosmetics
- Luggage
- Electronics

What Does Zappos Do to Retain Employees?

You will want to work here.

If you visit their website, you'll see that this company values fun and profit equally. A clear example that Zappos remains relevant is how they "blog out loud" on their website. You'll see postings for a desktop s'mores birthday party; Mannequin Monday; Pink Gorilla Guy photo ops; a visit from Duke, the mascot for the Las Vegas Wrangles ice hockey team; a kids' expo; a phony ATM machine that spits out redeemable "Zollars"; and a young man who built a cardboard house around his cubicle and is getting donated home furnishings to decorate it.

They Will Pay You to Quit?!

At the end of your first thirty days with the company, they offer you—and every new employee—a quitting bonus. Yes, they will pay almost $5,000 for you to walk away—to quit working for the company! They only want to keep people who *really* want to work there, so they don't want to invest more money into training you if you plan to leave anyway. This is a wildly innovative way to weed out the unenthusiastic employees.

Pay for Play?

But if you stay, you score.

Zappos appreciates hard work and isn't shy about sharing the wealth. At an all-employees meeting to discuss performance for 2007, Hsieh went over the year's financials and announced a surprise bonus. Imagine sitting in the audience when he says, "...for helping us beat our operating profit goals for 2007, each employee will receive a bonus check equal to 10 percent of whatever he or she made in 2007—roughly equivalent to five-and-a-half weeks of pay!"

The place erupted. The blog later was littered with grateful comments from employees sharing what they will do with that windfall, ranging from "make a down payment on a condo" to "save it," "buy a decent car," and "pay off all of my bills." Do you think anyone turned in a pink slip that day—or any other day, for that matter?

Is Their Culture Relevant?

Zappos perpetuates a culture of "wowness." One of the favorite phrases they bandy about is "Have a C.O.W.," which stands for Cultivators of Wowness. At Zappos, they celebrate random acts of wowness, which has a lot more punch than "random acts of kindness" because it is customer-oriented. They never lose sight of the customer's perspective—even when they aren't working.

Here's a great story I borrowed from the Zappos blog:

I stopped at Walgreens down the street. I had a ton of stuff to get. When I got to the register, two people got in line behind me. I let them both go first rather than wait on me. Then it was my turn. I was about a third of the way into being checked out when an older gentleman got in line. He had two cans of peanuts, some salve, and Chapstick. I turned to him and told him to give them to me. He had a strange look on his face and asked me why. I told him that I was going to pay for them so that he didn't have to wait for me to get checked out. He asked why. Out of my mouth came, "It's a random act of Wowness." I totally meant to say, "random act of kindness," but because of working here at Zappos, the word "WOW" came out. Rather than correct what I said, I just went with it. He handed me his items, I had the cashier scan them and put them in bag, and I gave them to the gentleman. He said, "Tell me about this 'random acts of Wowness.' I explained that it was doing nice things for people, even strangers. He was so grateful; he thanked me and left the store. Then the cashier asked me more about this "random acts of Wowness." I explained that I worked at Zappos and that we WOW our customers.

I feel that I shared this wowness with two people and that they BOTH will pay it forward (have you seen the movie, *Pay it Forward*?) I had such a great feeling when I left the store.

On Friday morning when I left here at 7:00 AM, I stopped in the same Walgreens. I had barely gotten in the door when I heard, "Hi, Martha!" I thought that someone from work was there. I looked around and realized that it was the same cashier from before.

I said to him, "I'm surprised that you remembered me and my name." He said "I wrote your name down from the credit card receipt, and of course I remember you, you're the person who told me about the 'random acts of wow or kindness.' He said that he had told other people about it!

It doesn't always mean paying for something for someone; many things you can do are free. Examples: bringing your neighbor's trash can back from the curb, bringing their newspaper to the door, opening a door for someone, or just putting a smile on someone's face.

—Martha C.

For the price of a couple of cans of peanuts and some Chapstick, Martha has created a growing army of unpaid marketing people to help spread the news about how Zappos generates "wowness."

Anyone want to argue that Zappos won't hit the billion-dollar mark soon?

My money is on Zappos.

Superstar Number Two: Bobbleheads and 90 Percent Annual Growth for Seventeen Straight Years

Start with nothing and get rich.

I was about to put this book to bed and send it off to the publisher when my son, Ryan, said, "Dad, do you know about BDA in Seattle, Washington?"

Having spent most of my adult life in that city, and being pretty well-acquainted with the major players in town, I was embarrassingly stumped.

"Nope, I haven't heard of them," I said.

Ryan pushed, "Better check them out, because they've averaged 90 percent growth over seventeen consecutive years."

My first assumption was that they must be a software company. I was wrong.

BDA, Inc., is a full-service merchandise company. They dominate the industry niche of companies hired to provide *your* company with customized premium items. In fact, there are more than twenty thousand such providers of giveaway key chains, conference buttons, logo sport shirts, and engraved pen sets. But to say that BDA toils in *that* space does a sore disservice to this inventive and innovative company.

They supply organizations with branded merchandise for sales promotions, sports and entertainment marketing, consumer products, and full blown e-commerce solutions. In fact, BDA is the number-one sports promotions company in the industry, with more than $300 million in annual revenue.

And they accomplished this from very humble beginnings.

In 1984, Eric Bensussen and Jay Deutsch were nineteen and sixteen years old, respectfully. The boys started their tiny business selling customized T-shirts at Seattle's annual Seafair hydroplane races. Seafair is a weeklong outdoor event that draws two hundred thousand-plus fans to the sunny August shores of Lake Washington, where they watch unlimited class hydroplanes spin the course at 190 miles per hour. The audience is captive, enthusiastic, and traditionally well-lubricated with suntan oil and beer. The boys' shirts were an instant hit. Buoyed by their success, they approached local aircraft design-and-build behemoth, Boeing Aircraft Co. Their idea was to design some logo sweatshirts. With a whopping order of 24 units, they squeezed themselves into the "big time" and had enough confidence to approach the newly formed Seattle Seahawk football club about licensing. It was early enough in the NFL properties business for the league to take a chance on a couple of kids. They printed T-shirts, rally rags, and hankies.

Then they came up with an idea that they could cross-pollinate from another industry. This was an idea that would revolutionize sports memorabilia forever.

Bobbleheads Were a Revolution?

Bobblehead dolls aren't new.

Bobblehead dolls had been around since the 1930s, but nobody had thought to create sports-hero bobblehead dolls. Deutsch and Bensussen immediately saw the sports application.

"We thought the dolls would be popular, but we didn't foresee the stampede. The press and lines of collectors formed around the stadium because we had stumbled onto an instant fad. I guess you could say that what we did right was that we thought the dolls could be collectible. So, we only produced twenty thousand units of each figure. Today, you can find them on eBay for outrageous sums."

Don't Be in the "Fad" Business

Fads don't last.

Relevant organizations can learn a huge lesson from BDA. Being relevant should be a state of mind that can nurse substantial profits from ongoing change—not constantly going for the quick score. While most organizations would be thrilled to have created an overnight sensation, these guys don't dwell on it. Deutsch relates, "We don't chase the 'shiny objects.' Everybody sees those faddish-type things. We've done specialized games for companies that became popular, but they never became an ongoing category for us. Our strength as a company was built on the idea that we want to create sustainable business concepts."

Deutsch continues, "Relevance for us is to focus on *not* becoming complacent. We don't bask in what we did yesterday, but rather concentrate on what we will be doing. What's new? That's exciting to us. You know, Eric and I are very engaged in this business. We are passionate and fired up to come to work, and curious about where the world is taking us, about the next level."

Asking for the Business

Because they were fearless about approaching the so-called "untouchable brands" with their outrageous ideas, the marketing community embraced BDA as an inventive partner.

In the '90s they had licensing for Batman, Superman, and Spiderman products, as well as Looney Tunes cartoons merchandise. What about pop culture? Nickelodeon, Star Wars, and the American Idol merchandise, to name just a few, are theirs as well. In fact, Eric and Jay have provided their promotional guidance to Fortune 500 companies, major Hollywood studios, Major League Baseball, the National Basketball Association, the National Hockey League, and the National Football League.

So the question I had for Deutsch was, "Why would Paramount Pictures hire you to manufacture and license these products? Wouldn't it be more profitable to do that sort of thing in-house?"

He told me, "We have the domestic and offshore manufacturing processes already in place and nailed. We have the creative people to provide fresh ideas for busy executives. It's what we do all day, every day. In fact, we are the missing unit from most companies' overall marketing mix. And since we work in tandem with other 'traditional agencies'—such as advertising and public relations firms—we don't pose a threat to their efforts. Our incredible buying power and shipping relationships give us an enormous pricing advantage over anyone else in our industry. Organizations such as Starbucks or Paramount would rather just approve the designs and let us do the heavy lifting. For them, the result is a fat residual check at the end of the day."

BDA Breathes Passion and Purpose

What impressed me most about Jay Deutsch during our phone interview was his absolute enthusiasm and passion for what they do at BDA. I could imagine working there and seeing his beaming face every day. He is infectious. He makes you feel good about the company. This is definitely a guy you would want to work for. If you visit their website (www.bdainc.com), you can get a quick glimpse into the BDA world when you see and hear Deutsch talk about how they see the power of merchandise as a marketing vehicle.

> We had the same idea twenty-four years ago that still holds true today. For people to truly connect with a brand, they need to touch it. They need to feel it. They need to interact with it. And it's complementary with what happens on the [TV or movie] screen, or in print or radio advertising. But to truly create a brand experience, people need to incorporate it into their lives. They need to pick it up and have a one-on-one connection with it. Now, this is what we call three-dimensional advertising. And, merchandise is at the absolute center of it!

Deutsch is making a brilliant case for promotional merchandise as an agent for emotion. Think about the last time you went to a ball game and somebody was waving a giant foam finger. That person is a champion of the brand. How about the last time you wore a T-Shirt or hat bearing the logo of your favorite musical act? You not only define who you are, but you have become an emotional extension of that brand. If you are the owner of that brand, you are ecstatic that someone wants to be your walking billboard.

But BDA wants to do more than build your brand awareness among your customers. They want you to view promotional merchandise as a way for you to make more money.

They Care About ROI and Relevance ...
With Their Customers

It's all about the money.

Return on investment (ROI) is the acid test of relevance with BDA's customers. Their Merchandise Agency^{SM} defines itself through specific ROI metrics. Delivering their clients a significant return on their investment in merchandise has set BDA apart from all its competitors. Deutsch told me, "We not only want to increase brand awareness, we want to turn these promotional products into a tangible consumer/client product—something you would be proud to wear, or put on your desk, and something that can actually become a profit center for your company."

Naturally, there is pressure to provide gross brand impressions. But BDA doesn't want you to think of merchandise as an expense. They want you to think of these products as a self-funding revenue stream. They know that cool merchandise tied to a real-time web store (that BDA can design for you) or a brick-and-mortar outlet will generate true dollars. Because their approach is very partner-esque, they have established an international reputation for backing up their ideas by sharing the risk.

The Michelin Man ...Goes Retail

As a testament to BDA's client commitment, they have opened a retail store in Greenville, South Carolina, featuring exclusively Michelin-brand merchandise. Is there a market for Michelin Man dolls and T-shirts? Deutsch said, "Yes. We believe so much in this concept that we put our own money on the line. All of the employees in that store are BDA employees."

But How Can You Measure the Success of a Merchandise Program?

Brand merchandise can—and should—be a profit center.

BDA has trademarked a program they call Environmental Affinity Impressions. The EAI is BDA's proprietary measurement tool dedicated to providing metrics for merchandise-based advertising. More importantly, though, the EAI measures the long-term affinity that develops between the customer and the branded merchandise. BDA is the only company of its kind who has the proprietary ability to measure the actual gross impressions and long-term affinity.

Yeah, But Does It Work?

Apparently, it works very well.

BDA has been recognized as one of the "Top Ten Merchandise Suppliers" in the promotional products industry, as well as the largest privately held sales promotions agency, according to *PROMO Magazine*. Their clients also have recognized BDA's efforts. Eli Lilly and Company named them the "Supplier of the Year" in 2007. Bank of America recognized BDA for their Women- and Minority-Owned Business Enterprises (WMBE) commitment.

Being Relevant to Their Employees

What may surprise you is that their $300 million revenue has been grown organically. BDA has never acquired another company to boost its top or bottom lines. This organization knows that finding and keeping great talent is the key to the ongoing growth of the company.

Other people have noticed, too.

In 2007, *Washington CEO Magazine* named BDA as one of the "Best Companies to Work for in Washington State." I asked Deutsch for his secret. He said, "For one thing, we have cultivated this culture from scratch and haven't had to meld it with another entity's culture. We make it a point to listen to everybody's ideas, regardless of the title on their business card. We value everyone. It's funny: when people come here to interview, they say they get a great 'vibe' just sitting in the lobby. When they start to walk around and meet people, the lasting impression is 'you've got some amazing people working here.' We also have two human resource VP's. One VP is in charge of family (internal), and works on career development within the organization. The other VP watches over company culture and environment. They are vigilant to make sure we are still connecting to our people. With eighteen offices around the United States, that's one of the best ways we can invest in our people."

(**Side note**: Prospective Zappos employees also go through the two-interview process. The first interview is to determine required skill sets. The second interview is about *culture fit*. Zappos wants to know if you are going to like working with the rest of their team—and if they will enjoy working with you.)

Consequently, at a time when most organizations are scrambling to find top talent, some of the best people working at BDA have come through referrals from existing staff. Good, smart people know other good, smart people.

Their philosophy has always been to find experts in their respective fields and treat them well. If you ask any of the 490 employees at BDA, they will tell you that the working environment is fueled by creativity, fun, and commitment Younger employees at BDA love the company's enthusiasm for staying relevant in the technology field. BDA was the first company in the promotions industry to offer truly real-time web stores. With one of the largest internal IT departments and hosting facilities in the industry, BDA has continued to establish its dominance in the e-shopping environment with their latest web store solution, YV5TM. Rather than try to decipher the origin of the code name, they explained to me that this proprietary software comes complete with real-time ordering capabilities and online product creation. BDA continues to set the standard for web store offerings.

Can You Replicate the BDA "Formula"?

One of the most interesting things I learned from Deutsch was that he and Bensussen didn't have any mentors along the way. They had something far more powerful: they had humility. They admit they've made plenty of mistakes in their twenty-four years together but they never tried to hide them. Deutsch says, "If you make a mistake around here, stand up and say so. Don't bury it. Don't dodge it. Admit it, and let's move on. Some people think that admitting a mistake is a sign of weakness. We coach people to admit that a mistake is a sign of strength."

Hmmm, 90 percent annual growth doesn't seem so far-fetched now, does it?

Relevant Review

If you glossed over any of the other chapters in this book, I won't be offended. But do me one favor, please. Reread this last chapter until you know it by heart and can tell the stories to your friends. These two companies should be a daily inspiration to you. I hope they nudge you to be better, more profitable, and kinder to your customers, clients, and patients. You see, I operate on the premise that *every* business has an opportunity to help strengthen a global economy. And I selfishly want the economy to keep growing so that when my young daughter finds her way into the workplace, she will have as many blossoming choices as we enjoy today.

It has been a thrill for me to relay what some organizations are doing to stay fresh and relevant because it's a thrill for them to talk about it. They would also be the first to tell you it is a daily struggle.

Remaining relevant requires you to work diligently and accept that the world never takes a day off. Relevancy requires 24/7 vigilance to your internal and external culture, technology, shifting operational methods, global influences, your competition's innovations, your available talent-pool's needs, and even the environment. But if your eyes and ears are open to change and you accept that adaptability is the cornerstone of your continued existence, you will thrive in any economy.

Those who don't take relevance seriously will follow other well-known brands into the corporate boneyard of extinction.

Those who stay relevant are a shining inspiration to all of us to keep improving, keep innovating, and to keep making life exciting and unpredictable.